Israel Lombard Jr,
from his friend
John Ayres,
Jany 1st 1862

PRAYERS

BY

THEODORE PARKER

BOSTON
WALKER, WISE AND COMPANY
1862

RIVERSIDE, CAMBRIDGE:
STEREOTYPED AND PRINTED BY H. O. HOUGHTON

To

THE WIFE OF THEODORE PARKER

This Volume of Prayers

IS AFFECTIONATELY DEDICATED

BY THE EDITORS.

PREFACE.

SINCE the death of our minister, many of his friends have expressed an earnest desire for the publication of some of his prayers, copies of which were secured during the whole period of his ministry at the Music Hall, and the latter half of that at the Melodeon, — caught in the air as they fell from the lips of the speaker, and faithfully daguerreotyped by friendly hands, and now choicely treasured. From these accumulations of so many years the forty prayers which are included in this volume have been selected, the one at the close being the last that Mr. Parker delivered in public.

A greater variety might have been given to the character of this volume by the insertion of other prayers, to the exclusion of some that it now contains; but it is thought that those here given best represent the earnest devotion and the highest aspirations of him who uttered them, presenting, as they do, those themes upon which he most loved to dwell, in sermon or in prayer; and while there is not a very wide range of topics included in the selection, it will be observed that there is much variety in the expression of ideas on the same topics.

The only alterations that have been made in the prayers as originally delivered are, the omission, here and there, of phrases often repeated, the introduction of a few passages from other prayers, and the correction of such slight errors of expression as are incidental to extemporaneous speaking.

It is believed that this little book will be dearly welcomed, not only by those at whose instance it has been prepared, but by thousands of others who have been "lifted up and strengthened" by these lofty utterances of a great and noble soul.

R. L.
M. G.

Boston, September 26, 1861.

PRAYERS.

I.

MARCH 17, 1850.

O THOU Infinite Spirit, who needest no words for man to hold his converse with thee, we would enter into thy presence, we would reverence thy power, we would worship thy wisdom, we would adore thy justice, we would be gladdened by thy love, and blessed by our communion with thee. We know that thou needest no sacrifice at our hands, nor any offering at our lips; yet we live in thy world, we taste thy bounty, we breathe thine air, and thy power sustains us, thy justice guides, thy goodness preserves, and thy love blesses us forever and ever. O Lord, we cannot fail to praise thee, though we cannot praise thee as we would. We bow our faces down before thee with humble hearts, and in thy presence would warm our spirits for a while, that the better we may be prepared for the duties of life, to endure its trials, to bear its crosses, and to triumph in its lasting joys.

We thank thee for the world that is about us, now

serene, enlightened by the radiance of day, now covered over with clouds and visited by storms, and in serenity and in storm still guarded and watched and blessed by thee. We adore thee who givest us all these things that we are, and promisest the glories that we are to become. For our daily life we thank thee, for its duties to exercise our hands, for its trials and temptations to make strong our hearts, for the friends that are dear to us, — a joy to us in our waking hours, and in the visions of the night still present, and a blessing still.

We thank thee, O Lord, for thy tender providence which is over us all, for thy loving kindness which blesses the child and the old man, which regards the sinner with affection, and lovest still thine holy child. Father, we know that we are wanderers from thy way, that we forget thy laws, that oft-times the world has dominion over us, that we are slaves to passion and to every sense. And yet we rejoice to remember that thy kindness is not as our kindness, and thy love is infinite, that thou tenderly carest for thy children, that thou art the Shepherd of the sheep, and in thy bosom bearest the feeble lambs, and gently leadest at last each wanderer back to its home.

We pray thee that we may forgive ourselves for every sin we commit, that with penitence we may wash out the remembrance of wrong, and with wings of new resolution fly out of darkness in the midst of transgression, into the higher, brighter heaven of human duty, of human joy, and of the Christian's peace.

Teach us, O Lord, to use this world wisely and faithfully and well. In its daily duties and its trials may we find the school for wisdom, for goodness, and for piety. May we learn by every trial that thou sendest, be strengthened by every cross, and when we stoop in sadness to drink bitter waters, may we rise refreshed and invigorated. Help us to live at peace with our souls, disturbing no string on this harp of a thousand chords, but attuning all to harmony, and in our life living one great triumphant hymn to thee. Withhold from us what is evil, though we beg mightily for it, and with tears and prayers. Help us to live in unity with our brother men, reconciling our interest to their interests, by faithfully discharging every duty, by patiently bearing with the weakness or the strength of our brothers, and loving them as we love ourselves. Teach us, Father, to love the unlovely, to love those who evil entreat us, to toil for those who are burdens in the world, and to seek to save them from ignorance, to reform them of their wickedness, and to hasten that time when all men shall recognize that thou art their Father, and their brothers are indeed their brothers, and that all owe fidelity to thee and loving-kindness to their fellow-men. Help us to live in unity with thee, no sloth hiding us from thy presence, no passion turning us aside from thy counsel, but, with mind and conscience, with heart and soul, assimilating ourselves to thee, till thy truth dwells in our understanding, and thy justice enlightens our conscience, and thy love shines a beatitude and a blessed light in our heart and soul forever and ever.

In times of darkness, when men fail before thee, in days when men of high degree are a lie, and those of low degree are a vanity, teach us, O Lord, to be true before thee, not a vanity, but soberness and manliness; and may we keep still our faith shining in the midst of darkness, the beacon-light to guide us over stormy seas to a home and haven at last. Father, give us strength for our daily duty, patience for our constant or unaccustomed cross, and in every time of trial give us the hope that sustains, the faith that wins the victory and obtains satisfaction and fulness of joy.

Our Father who art in heaven, hallowed be thy name. May thy kingdom come, and thy will be done on earth as it is done in heaven. Give us each day our daily bread. Forgive us our trespasses as we forgive those who trespass against us. Lead us not into temptation, but deliver us from its evil. For thine is the kingdom, and the power, and the glory forever. Amen.

II.

AUGUST 4, 1850.

O THOU Eternal One, whose presence fills all space and occupies all time, who hast thy dwelling-place in every humble heart that trustfully looks up to thee, we flee to thee again to offer thee our morning psalm of thanksgiving and of praise, and to ask new inspiration from thee for days to come, while we stain our sacrifice with penitence for evils that our hands have wrought. Father, may thy spirit pray with us in our prayer, teaching us the things that we ought to ask of thee; may we serve thee faithfully and worship thee aright. O Lord, we bow down our spirits before thee, we reverence thine infinite power, we adore thine unbounded wisdom, which understands things past, things present, and to come; we confide in thy perfect justice, knowing that we are safe; but, O Lord, we rejoice in thy love. We bless thee for thy tender mercies, our hearts thank thee for thy loving-kindness, and we reach out the arms of our soul towards thee, knowing that thou art our Father, who lovest us better even than the mothers that have borne us. O Lord, we do not know how to praise thee as we ought, for we do not understand all of thy goodness, we cannot measure all of thy loving-kindness towards us, for it is infinite.

We thank thee for the signs and tokens of thyself which thou hast placed around us everywhere. We thank thee for this lovely day which thou lendest us. We bless thee for the broad green world beneath our feet, for these wondrous heavens above our heads, which nightly thou sowest with starry seed, and every morning limnest with orient light. We thank thee that all these things are a revelation of thee, for day giveth voice unto day, and night speaketh unto night, and the rivers as they roll, and the ocean as it ebbs and floods, and this all-embracing sky, — O Lord, they tell of thy magnitude, they speak of thy power, they talk of thy wisdom, and they charm us with tidings of thy love.

But a greater revelation than this of thyself hast thou made in thy still small voice, which whispers in our soul that all this magnificence is but a drop of thee, yea, a little sparklet that has fallen from thy presence, thou Central Fire, and Radiant Light of all. We know that these outward things are but a sparkle of thy power, a whisper of thy wisdom, a faint breath of thy loving-kindness. O Lord, we thank thee that on our soul thou hast writ that thou art our Father, that thy name is Love, that we should not tremble nor fear before thee, but as a child to its mother, so may we turn longingly and lovingly and with unfailing trust to thee. Pardon us that we have known thee no better, that we have trembled when we should have rejoiced, and have been afraid when there was none to molest us nor to make us afraid. O Lord, open our inner eye that we may see thee as thou art, touch thou our soul with thine own inspiration that we may know thee, that we may love thee, that we may serve thee with our daily life.

We remember in our prayer the temptations which every day brings with it, our sorrows, and our trials, and our cares. Arm us for the duty which thou givest us to do, make us strong to bear every cross, patient and earnest to do every day's work in its own day, and to bear ourselves so bravely that we shall always acquit us as men, and so be strong. In our day of passion, we pray thee to deliver us out of its flame and heat, that we come as thy children of old out of the furnace, with no smell of its pollution on our garment's hem. And in the more dangerous period of interest and ambition, we pray thee to save us from its chilling cold and its wintry frost, that we come out not benumbed by its palsy, nor frozen by its snow. Give us wisdom to disperse our darkness, let justice triumph over selfishness in our soul, let duty be supreme over desire, till every desire becomes dutiful and our daily life is one continual sacrament to thee. Father, let a living love of thee dwell in our hearts, let it become strong within us, and lead to a faith that fails not and needs not to be ashamed. May our earthly life be beautiful and acceptable in thy sight, and may our souls be filled with every spiritual gift from thee; and receiving much, may we give the more, making our lives still more acceptable to thee. Lead us through evil and through good report, bearing the cross which thou layest upon us; and by our prayers, our toil and our tears, change thou us into the glorious image of thyself, that we may be wholly thine, transformed to thee, and thy truth dwell with us, thy justice pitch her tent with us, and thine own loving-kindness charm and enchant our very souls. So may thy kingdom come, and so thy will be done on earth as it is done in heaven.

III.

OCTOBER 6, 1850.

OUR Father who art in heaven, thou Soul of our souls, and Safeguard of the world, we flee to thee to sing our morning psalm, to pray our morning prayer, bringing the offering of gratitude from our hearts, and asking of thee the gift of thy holy spirit. Thou sendest down thy sunlight on the world, thou rainest thy rain to still the dust and pacify the stones of the street crying for moisture from the skies, and we know that thou wilt feed our spirits with thine inspiration, ministering truth to the hungry mind, justice to the conscience that asketh right of thee, and wilt pour thy holy love on every earnest, seeking, asking soul.

We thank thee for thy broad providence which cares for the grass in the fields, and adorns every little flower that fringes the hedgerows of life, and carest also for the mighty orbs above our heads and the solid ground beneath our feet; and thyself art not hard to find, nor far to seek, but art with every living soul of man. Father, we thank thee for thy justice which presides over this world, and out of evil bringeth forth good continually, disappointing the wickedness of men, and doing all things for our good. We thank thee for thine unbounded love which caused us to be, which made this fair world, which waiteth for us in our transgressions, and goes out to meet us, prodigals or penitent, a great way off, and blesses still thy wandering, even unrepentant child. We thank thee for thy voice in our hearts, for the inspiration which thou givest to the sons of men, to show us the way in which we should go, to rebuke us for every folly, to chastise us for every sin, but to encourage everything that is holy and noble and true in our hearts.

We thank thee for the noble examples of human excellence which thou raisest up from time to time, the landmarks of human life, and our guiding lights to lead us safely home to port and peace, to heaven here and heaven at last with thee.

We pray thee that we may be faithful and true to every gift which thou hast given us. In a time of darkness, when great men are a deceit and little men are a lie, may our heart never fail us, nor we hesitate nor despair for a moment of thy goodness and thy truth. Though hand join in hand, teach us that wickedness cannot prosper, nor iniquity endure. Fix our eyes on the true, the right, the holy, the beautiful, and the good, till we love them, and therein love thee with an affection that cannot be ashamed and will not be defeated. Teach us to be blameless in our daily life, to be heroic in our conduct, distinguishing between the doctrines of men and thine everlasting commandments. Help us to love thee, the Creator, more than the creature before our eyes; to imitate thy justice, to share thy truth, and to spread abroad thy living love to all mankind. Are we weak, — and we know we are, — give us strength; sinners, — and our heart cries out against us, — chastise and rebuke us till we repent of our sin, and come back with humble hearts to worship thee in holiness, in nobleness, and in truth. Give us the love of thyself which shall tread down every passion under its feet that wars against the soul, that shall make our daily lives beneficent, and so cast out every fear, the fear of man, and the fear, O Lord, of thee. Help us to know thee in thine immensity, to feel thee and to love thee in thine infinite love, till every weight is cast off from us, and with thy sunshine on our wings we mount up as eagles and fly towards thee. We pray that we may be armed against temptation, and fortified inly for every duty, prepared for every emergency, and ready to serve thee with our limbs and our lives.

We ask thy blessing on all sorts and conditions of men in the various departments of our mortal lives. May the young be trained up in innocence, and taught, not to fear men, but to love their brothers and to love thee. When sundered but joyful souls are by their affection wedded and made one, may a higher life spring up in their united hearts, and may they serve thee with blameless beauty and celestial piety set in a mortal life. In the various trials of our daily business teach us to be honest, and to love men, to respect the integrity of our own souls, and never waver, turned this side by the fear of men, and that side by the lust for their praise and their admiration.

We remember the poor and the needy in our prayer; yea, Lord, the poorest and the neediest of all, who own not by human laws their bodies, nor their limbs, nor lives, who flee from the iron house of bondage and ask shelter here with us. Yea, Lord, their prayer from our lips goes up before thee, asking the rights of man which thou didst give them at their birth, but the oppressor so fraudfully and forcibly rent away. O Lord, we are all sinners before thee, but we remember those who with unashamed countenance tread down thy law, who even here seek for the life and freedom of men, and defile the fair heritage which our fathers asked of thee in their prayer and purchased with their sacred blood. Father, we pray thee that thou wilt pity those who have shown no pity, and wilt love those who to their brothers show only hate, treading them with bloody hoofs into the ground, and who with the brow of brass affront thy thunders and blaspheme thy love. Teach us, O Lord, our hardest task, to love also these. And our poor brothers, who with chained hands lift up an unchained soul to thee, who flee from city to city, while their persecutors desecrate thy name, who wander from one nation to another kingdom, seeking for the rights of man, — we pray thee that thou wilt guide them in their flight by night, and still by day, and raise up defenders for them here and everywhere. Stir up the souls of noble men that they bewray not him that wandereth, that they hide and shelter the outcast, and are a wall of fire about those who have taken their life in their hands and fled to us for succor, till a band of brothers fold their arms about the needy, and uplift those that are faint and ready to perish in their fall.

O Lord, thy charity never faileth. Touch the hearts of men with humanity, that they may learn justice and to love their brothers. Make us nobler, and braver, and holier. Teach us to love all men. So let us be thy children, loving those that hate us, and praying for such as despitefully use us. So may thy kingdom come, and thy will be done on earth as it is in heaven.

IV.

JULY 18, 1852.

OUR Father who art in heaven, who also art not less on earth, peopling every point of space with thy presence, and filling every point of spirit with thy power, thy wisdom, and thy love, we would lift up our souls unto thee, and gather together our scattered and estrayed spirits, that we may hold communion with thee for a moment in our prayer, and be strengthened for daily duty, and made newly grateful for joys which thou givest us, more faithful to ourselves and more reliant upon thee.

We know that thou wilt remember us, nor needest thou to be entreated in our morning psalm or morning prayer, for before our heart knows our need of thee, thou art with our heart, and sustainest and givest us life. Father, we know that though earthly friends may prove faithless, though distance of space and length of time may hide the child from the mother that bore him, yet thine eye never slumbers nor sleeps, and thou rememberest us when mortal friends forsake us, or when time and distance shut out the affections of the mortal heart. Yea, Lord, the distance is no distance with thee, for thy presence shineth everywhere as the day, and thy loving-kindness waits on the footsteps of morning, and thou fillest up the shades of evening, and givest to thy beloved, even in their sleep.

Father in heaven, we thank thee for all this world of thy providence, so fertile in wonders, so rich in beauty to every hungering sense of man. We thank thee that thou carest for the ground, that nightly thou waterest it with dews from heaven, and in thine own season sendest the river of waters in plenteous showers to moisten field and garden and hill and town. Father, we thank thee for thy loving-kindness and thy tender mercy, that thou watchest over every little fly spreading his thin wings in this morning's sun, and holdest this system of universes in thine own arms of infinite and never-ending love.

We thank thee for the beauty which thou bringest forth in every stream of water, on every hill-side, and that wherewith thou fringest the paths of men as they pass to their daily work. We bless thee for the beauty which thou gatherest in the lily's fragrant cup, clothing it with a kinglier loveliness than Solomon in all his glory could ever put on; and in these flowers of earth, and in those imperishable flowers of beauty over our heads, we read, O Lord, the alphabet of thy loving-kindness and thy tender mercy. But we thank thee still more that in a tenderer and lovelier and holier way thou revealest thy loving-kindness and thy tenderness and thy holiness of heart to thy children.

We thank thee for the large faculties with which thou hast gifted the children of men. We thank thee for the senses that take hold of the world of sight and touch and sound, and are fed and beautified thereon. We thank thee for these spiritual powers which lay hold of justice and truth, and love and faith in thee, these flowers of the soul, these imperishable stars of the human spirit; and we bless thee for thy yet greater loving-kindness and tender mercy which thou speakest to our souls. We thank thee that, as thou feedest the little grass by the roadside and every flower of the field with dew by night and rain by day, and warmest and waterest their roots, so thine inspiration falls down upon the souls of thy children, and thou feedest this strong and flamelike flower with thine own wisdom, thine own justice, thy holiness and thy love.

Lord, what shall we render to thee for the least of the mercies which thou hast given us? We pray thee that we may live as blameless as the flowers of the field; that our lives within may be as fragrant, and without as fair, and that what is promise in our spring, what is blossom in our summer, may in the harvest of heaven bear fruit of everlasting life.

We look unto thee, and we will not pray thee that thou wilt remember us. We know that though a mother may forget the babe that she has borne, thou never forsakest a single child of thine. In sorrow we turn our eyes to thee, and thou wipest the tears from our eyelids; in darkness we look up to thee, and it is all light within our soul. When those that are nearest and dearest to our heart have gone down to the sides of the pit, O Lord, we know that the mortal is rendered up that the soul may be clothed with immortality, and inherit everlasting joys with thee. When our own heart cries out against us, we know that thou art greater than our heart, and no folly, no wandering, and no sin can ever hide us from thine infinite motherliness. We bless thee that all thine ordinances are designed for our good, that the rod of thine affliction and the staff of our support, they both comfort us, for thou still art our shepherd, and leadest us beside the still waters, and wilt feed us in the full pastures and give peace to our soul.

O Thou our God, we pray thee that we may be strengthened for every day's duty, have patience to bear any cross that is laid upon us, wisdom to order our pathway aright, the heart of holiness to trust thee with an absolute faith, and the soul that is full of loving-kindness to do good to our brothers here on the earth. So may thy kingdom come, and thy will be done on earth as it is in heaven.

V.

AUGUST 1, 1852.

O THOU Creating and Protecting Power, who art our Father, yea, our Mother not the less, we flee unto thee, and would lift up the psalm of our thanksgiving unto thee, and by our prayer seek to hold communion with thy spirit, and be strengthened for the cares and the duties and the delights of our mortal life. We come before thee, O Lord, with the remembrance of our daily toils, and the common things of life still murmuring in our ears, and we would lift up our souls unto thee, to learn new wisdom, to acquire more justice, to feel a deeper philanthropy and a heartier piety in our own souls. We know that thou art not to be worshipped as though thou askedst even prayer at our poor lips, for we know that thou ever watchest over us, and foldest the universe in thine arms of love, needing no prayer of ours to kindle thy sympathy to the humblest of thy creatures. O Lord, the earth is thine altar, and the heavens over our head, they are the incense of creation offered in their beauty to thy greatness and thy glorious name. O Lord, the universe is a voice of thanksgiving unto thee, and in serene and cloudy days this flying globe lifts up her voice, and sings to thee, morning and evening and at noon of day, her continual psalm of joy and praise. But our hearts in their poverty constrain us to flee unto thee, out of the sorrows and the joys of this world, to praise thee for thy blessings, and to ask of thee new glories in time to come. We desire to be deeply conscious of thy presence, which fills all time, which occupies all space. We would know thee as thou art, and in our souls feel continually thy residence with us and the abiding of thy spirit in our heart.

Father, we thank thee for this wondrous and lovely world in which thou hast placed us. For the magnificent beauty of summer we thank thee, for the storied promise of the spring which has gone by, and the earnest of the harvest, whose weeks in their fulfilment bring daily new tokens of thy goodness and thine infinite love. We thank thee that thou waterest the earth with rain from thine own sweet heavens, rejoicing the cattle on a thousand hills, which thou also carest for, as for thy chosen ones, and ministerest life to every little moss amid the stones of a city, and feedest the mighty forests which clothe with verdure our own New England hills. We thank thee that thou givest us grass for the cattle, and corn to strengthen the frame of man, and orderest all things by number and measure and weight, wielding the whole into a mighty mass of usefulness and a glorious orb of transcendent beauty. We bless thee for the beautiful amid the homely, the sublime among things low, for the good amid evil things, and the eternal amid what is transient, and daily passing from our eye.

We thank thee for the happiness that attends us in our daily life, for the joys of our daily work, for the success which thou givest to the labors of our hand, and the strength to our soul which comes from our daily toil on the earth. We thank thee for the plain and common household joys of life, for the satisfactions of friendship, for the blessedness of love in all the dear relationships of mortal life. Father, we thank thee for the large sympathy with our brother-men everywhere, and that we know that thou hast made them all alike in thine own image, and hast destined all thy children to toil on the earth, and to a glorious immortality of never-ending blessedness beyond the grave.

Father, we thank thee that we know thee, that amid hopes that so often deceive us, amid expectations that fail and perish, we have still our faith assured in thee, who art without variableness or shadow of turning. O Lord, thou delightest us still more when we remember that our life itself is the gift of thine hand. In our sorrow and sadness we look up to thee, and when mortal friends fail us, and the urn that held our treasured joys is broken into fragments, and the wine of life is scattered at our feet, O Lord, we rejoice to know that thou understandest our lot, and wilt make every sorrow of our life turn out for our endless welfare, and our continual growth, so that thou wilt take us home to thyself with no stain of weeping on our face. O Lord, when ourselves have been false, when our own hearts cry out against us, and we stain our daily sacrifice with remorseful tears, we rejoice to know that thou art greater than our heart, and wilt bring home every wandering child of thine, with no stain of sin on our immortal soul. Father, we thank thee that amid the joys of the flesh, amid the delights of our daily work, and all the sweet and silent blessedness of mortal friendship and love upon the earth, thou givest us the joy of knowing thee, the still and calm delight of lying low in thy hand, and feeling the breath of thy spirit upon us. Yea, Lord, we thank thee that thou holdest each one of us, yea, all of thy children, and the universe itself, as a mother folds her baby to her bosom, and blessest us all with thine infinite loving-kindness and thy tender mercy.

O Father, we pray thee that we may never be false to the great glories with which thou surroundest us, under our feet, and over our head, and the still diviner glories which thou placest in our heart and soul. We pray thee that within us our lives may be blameless, every faculty active and at its work, and that our outward lives may be useful, and all our existence blameless and beautiful in thy sight, O Lord, our Strength and our Redeemer. May our lives be marked every day by some new lesson that we have learned, some duty that we have done, some faithfulness that we have accomplished; and at last, when our mortal pilgrimage is ended, take us to thyself, O Lord, to dwell with thee, leaving behind us the memory of good deeds, and bearing with us a soul disciplined by the trials of life, and enlarged by its blessings. So may we pass from glory to glory, till we are changed into thine own image, and the peace of thy love is made perfect in us. So may thy kingdom come, and thy will be done on earth as it is in heaven.

VI.

JULY 17, 1853.

OUR Father who art in heaven, who fillest all time with thine eternity and all space with thy loving-kindness and thy tender mercy, we flee unto thee once more, seeking to deepen our consciousness of thee, to pour out our hearts' gratitude for thy daily blessings continually given unto us, and to seek new inspiration from thy spirit, extending everywhere.

O Father, we thank thee for this world about us, and above us, and underneath our feet, which thou hast given us to dwell in. We thank thee for the ground that we tread on, for the trees that roof us over, for the bread that we eat, and for the fleeces that we wear.

Father, we thank thee for all this wonderful beauty wherein thou speakest to the wakening sense of man. We bless thee for the day, which from thy golden urn thou pourest out upon the world, and that every morning thou baptizest anew each speck of earth with heaven's own light. We thank thee that thou whitenest the darkness of the night by the moon's untiring beauty, and that thou pasturest the stars in thine own fields of boundless space, nor sufferest thou a single fleece of light ever to be lost, thou Shepherd of the earth, and Shepherd of the sky.

We thank thee for this nobler world of man, for its serener day, its light more heavenly, and all the blessed stars of consciousness that shine within our soul. We thank thee, that thou makest us capable to understand the material world that is about us, and to rule and master by wisdom, by justice and by love, this greater, nobler world that we are.

We thank thee for the still and silent joys that come to every earnest and holy heart. We bless thee for the happiness that attends our daily work, and all the things which thou givest us to do here on the earth.

We thank thee, that thou hast given us this immortal soul, which, feeding on the earth, grows for what is more than earthly, and with great hungering of heart, reaches ever upwards for what is perfect, for what is good and beautiful and holy in thine own sight. We thank thee that, as thou feedest every plant with dew from heaven, and with light from the world's great sun, so with sweet influence thou rainest inspiration down upon thy children, and with thy loving-kindness wilt bless every soul, though wandering oft-times from thee.

We remember before thee our daily lives, the perplexities of our business, the trials of our patience, the doubts, and the darkness, yea, and the sin that doth most easily beset us; and we pray thee that we may be warned by all that we suffer, and urged onwards by everything that we enjoy, till we have cast behind us the littleness of our childhood, and with manly, womanly dignity, pursue our march on earth, not weary though we run, and not fainting as we mount up like eagles towards thy perfection.

We remember before thee the disappointments, the sadness, and the affliction of our mortal life. We remember how often our arms are folded around emptiness, when the mortal whom we truly love has taken wings to itself and is immortal with thee.

Father, we pray thee, that thou wilt instruct us in these, our earthly misfortunes, and, by every disappointment, and all affliction, may we grow wiser, and purer, more holy-hearted still; and while in our feebleness we may not thank thee for what thou hast taken, O Lord, let us learn from sorrow a deeper lesson than joy and gladness ever bring. Even as the night reveals a whole heaven of stars, so may the darkness of disappointment, the night of sorrow, open heaven to thy children's eyes, till brighter beams are about us, and the consciousness of immortality fills up our souls and wipes the tears from every eye.

So may all our mortal life be a journey upwards, and we fly forwards towards thee, till, at last, may thy truth fill our understanding, may thy justice enlarge our heart, and may love and holiness and faith in thee subdue every unholy thing, and change us anew to thine own image, O Thou who art our Father and the Mother of our souls. So may thy kingdom come, and thy will be done on earth as it is in heaven.

VII.

FEBRUARY 5, 1854.

OUR Father who art in heaven, and on earth, and near unto every heart, we flee unto thee, seeking to feel thy presence, and, conscious of thee, to know thee as thou art, and to worship thee with all our mind and conscience and heart and soul. We seek to commune with thy spirit for a moment, that we may freshen our hearts, tired with the world's journey and sore travel, and bow our faces down and drink again at the living waters of thy life. O Thou Infinite One, we reverence thee, who art the permanent in things that change, the foundation of what lasts, the loveliness of things beautiful, and the wisdom and the justice and the love which make and hold and bless all this world of matter and of men. O Thou who art without variableness or turning shadow, we thank thee that thou needest not our poor prayers to teach thee of our need, nor askest thou our supplication's argument to quicken thy mercy or to stir thy love. Thou anticipatest before we call, and doest more and better for us than we can ever ask or think.

O Father, who adornest the summer and cheerest

the winter with thy presence, we thank thee that we know that thou art our Father, and our Mother, that thou foldest in thine arms all the worlds which thou hast made, and warmest with thy mother's breath each mote that peoples the sun's beams, and blessest every wandering, erring child of man.

O Lord, how marvellous is thy loving-kindness and thy tender mercy, which thou spreadest out over matter and beast and man. In loving-kindness hast thou made them all, and in tender mercy thou watchest over the wanderings of the world, blessing those that sorrow, and recalling such as go astray. Oh, whither can we flee from thy presence? If we take the wings of the morning, and dwell in the uttermost parts of the sea, even there shall thy hand lead us, and thy right hand shall hold us up. Yea, Lord, our transgression hideth us not from thee; but thine eye seeth in sin as in righteousness, and when our own hearts cry out against us, thou, who art greater than our heart, still takest us up, bearest us on thy wings, and blessest us with thine infinite love.

Father, we remember before thee our several wants and conditions in life, and we thank thee for the happiness that crowns our days, for the success that attends our efforts here on earth, the brightness that we gather in our homes, and the hearts whose beating is the music round our fireside and their countenance the blessing on our daily bread. We thank thee for these things wherein our hearts rejoice.

But we remember also in our prayer the world's sternness and severity, the sorrows that stain our face with weeping, and make our hearts sometimes run over with our sadness, and our deep distress. Father, if we cannot thank thee for the things that we suffer, we still will thank thee that we know that thine eye pities us in our sorrows, and no sadness stains our face but thou knewest it before we were born, and gatherest the tears which we shed, and changest them into glorious pearls, to shine in our crown of glory as morning stars that herald the coming of the heavenly kingdom here below.

We pray thee that we may find comfort in every sorrow, and when the world turns its cold, hard eye upon us, when the mortal fades from our grasp, and the shadow of death falls on the empty seat of child or wife or friend, O Lord, by the shining of thy candle in our heart, may we see our way through darkness unto light, and journey from strength to strength, our hearts still stayed on thee.

Help us to grow stronger and nobler by this world's varying good and ill, and while we enlarge the quantity of our being by continual life, may we improve its kind and quality not less, and become fairer, and tenderer, and heavenlier too, as we leave behind us the various events of our mortal life. So, Father, may we grow in goodness and in grace, and here on earth attain the perfect measure of a complete man. And so in our heart, and our daily life, may thy kingdom come, and thy will be done on earth as it is done in heaven.

VIII.

NOVEMBER 27, 1856.

THANKSGIVING DAY.

O THOU Infinite Spirit, who art everywhere that the light of day sheds down its glorious lustre, and in the caverns of the earth where the light of day cometh not, we would draw near to thee and worship thy spirit, which at all times is near to us. O Thou Infinite One, who art amidst all the silences of nature, and forsakest us not with thy spirit where the noisy feet of men are continually heard, we pray thee that the spirit of prayer may be in us while we lift up our hearts unto thee. Thou askest not even our gratitude, but when our cup is filled with blessings to the brim and runneth over with bounties, we would remember thee who fillest it, and givest every good and precious gift.

Father, we thank thee for the special material blessings which we enjoy; for the prosperity which has attended the labors of thy children in the months that are past, for the harvest of corn and of grass which the hand of man, obedient to his toilsome thought, has gathered up from the surface of the ground. We bless thee that when our toil has spoken to the earth, the furrows of the field have answered with sufficient, yea, with abundant returns of harvest to our hand. We thank thee for the blessings of the deep, and treasures hid in the sands, which thy children have gathered. We bless thee for the success which has come to those who go down to the sea in ships and do business in great waters. We thank thee for the treasures which our mining hand has gathered from the foldings of the earth, the wealth which we have quarried from the mountain, or digged out from the bosom of the ground. And we bless thee for the other harvests which from these rude things the toilsome hand and the laborious thought of men have created, turning use into beauty also, and so adorning and gladdening the world.

We thank thee for the special blessings that come near to us this day. We bless thee for the health of our bodies, and we thank thee for those who are near and dear to us; and for all the gladsome gatherings together which this day will bring to pass, of parents and their children, long severed, or of the lover and his beloved, who so gladly would become one. We bless thee for all those who this day shall break their bread in common, lifting up their hearts unto thee, and blessing the hand which lengthens out our days and keeps the golden bowl from breaking at the fountain; and we thank thee for those who in many a distant place are still of us,—severed in the body, but with us yet in soul.

We remember before thee not only our families and

our homes, but likewise the great country in which thou hast cast the lines of our lot. We thank thee for its wide extent, for the great riches which the toil of man has here gathered together and stored up. We bless thee for the multitudes of people, an exceeding great company of men and women, who here have sprung into existence under thy care. We bless thee that in this land the exile from so many a clime can find a home, with none to molest nor to make him afraid. We thank thee for every good institution which has here been established, for all the truth that is taught in the church, for what of justice has become the common law of the people, and for all of righteousness and of benevolence which goes forth in the midst of our land.

We bless thee for our fathers who in centuries past, in the name of thy holy spirit, and for the sake of rights dearest to mankind, went from one country to another people, and in their day of small things came here. Yea, we thank thee for those whose only communion was an exile, and we bless thee for the bravery of their spirit which would not hang the harp on the willow, but sung songs of thanksgiving in a strange land, and in the midst of their wilderness builded a new Zion up, full of thanksgiving and song and praise.

We bless thee for our fathers of a nearer kin, who in a day of peril strove valiantly that they might be free, and bequeathed a noble heritage to their sons and daughters who were to come after them. Yea, we thank thee for those whose sacrament was only a revolution, and the cup of blessing was of blood drawn from their own manly veins; and we bless thee for the hardy valor which drew their sword, and sheathed it not till they had a large place, and their inalienable rights secured to them by their own right hand, toiling and striving under the benediction of thy precious providence. Now, Lord, we thank thee that the few have become a multitude, and the little vine which our fathers planted with their tears and watered with their blood, reaches from sea to sea, great clusters of riches hanging on every bough, and its root strong in the land.

But we remember before thee the great sins which this nation has wrought, and while we thank thee for the noblest heritage which man ever inherited from man, we must mourn also that we have blackened the ground with crimes such as seldom a nation has committed against thee. Yea, Lord, even our thanksgiving prayer must be stained with our tears of mourning, and our psalm of thanksgiving must be mingled with the wail of those who lament that they have no hope left for them in the earth. Father, we remember our brothers of our own kin and complexion whom wickedness has smitten down in another land, whose houses are burned and their wives given up to outrage. We remember those who walk only in chains this day, and are persecuted for their righteousness' sake. And still more in our prayer we remember the millions of our brothers whom our fathers chained, and whose fetters our wicked hands have riveted upon their limbs. O Lord, we pray thee that we may suffer from these our transgressions, till we learn to eschew evil, to break the rod of the oppressor, and to let the oppressed go free; yea, till we make our rulers righteousness, and those chief amongst us whose glory it is to serve mankind by justice, by fidelity, and by truth.

We pray thee, on this day of our gratitude, that we may rouse up everything that is humanest in our heart, pledging ourselves anew to do justly and to love mercy, and to walk humbly before thee, O Thou our Father and our Mother on earth and in the heavens too. Thus, Lord, may our thanksgiving be worthy of the nature thou hast given us and the heritage thou hast bequeathed. Thus may our psalm of gratitude be a hymn of thanksgiving for millions who have broken off their chains, and for a great country full of joy, of blessedness, of freedom and of peace. So may thy kingdom come and thy will be done on earth as it is in heaven.

IX.

DECEMBER 28, 1856.

O THOU Infinite One, who fillest the ground under our feet and the heavens over our head, whither shall we go from thy spirit or whither shall we flee from thy presence? If we take the wings of the morning and dwell in the uttermost parts of the sea, even there shall thy hand lead us, and thy right hand shall hold us up. If we say, Surely the darkness shall cover us, even the darkness shall be light about us; yea, the darkness hideth not from thee, but the darkness and the light are both alike to thee.

Father, we know that at all times and in every place thou wilt remember us, nor askest thou the persuasive music of our morning hymn, nor our prayer's poor utterance, to stir thy loving-kindness towards us; for thou carest for us when sleep has sealed our senses up and we heed thee no more; yea, when enveloped in the smoke of human ignorance or of folly, thine eye is still upon us, thou understandest our needs, and doest for us more and better than we are able to ask, or even to think. But in our feebleness and our darkness, we love to flee unto thee, who art the light of all our being, the strength of all which is strong, the wisdom of what is wise, and the foundation of all things that are; and while we lift up our prayer of aspiration unto thee, and muse on thy presence with us, and the various events of our life, the fire of devotion must needs flame in our heart, and gratitude dwell on our tongue.

Father, we thank thee for the world about us and above and beneath. We bless thee for the austere loveliness of the wintry heavens, for those fixed or wandering fires which lend their splendor to the night, for the fringe of beauty wherewith thou borderest the morning and the evening sky, and for this daily sun sending his roseate flush of light across the white and wintry world. We thank thee for all the things that are kindly to our flesh, which our toil has won from out the brute material world.

We bless thee for all the favorable things that are about us; for those near and dear to us, whom we watch over, and those who long since watched over and blessed us. We thank thee for wise words spoken to us in our childhood or our youth, for the examples of virtue which were round us, and for the tender voice which spoke to our spirit in early days, and wakened in us a sense of reverence, of love and of trust in thy spirit. We thank thee for the fathers and mothers who bore us, for the kinsfolk, the friends, the acquaintance, and the teachers, who brought us reverently up; for all the self-denial which watched over our cradles, which held our head when our heart was sick, sheltering us from the world's hardness, holding up our childish hands when they hung down, and guiding our tottering footsteps when we ran giddy in the paths of youth. Yea, we thank thee for all the examples of excellence, the words of kindly remonstrance and virtuous leading, which have been a lamp to our path, showing us the way in which we should go.

We thank thee for the noble institutions which have come down to us; for the church, with its many words of truth and its recollections of ancient piety; for the state, with its wise laws; for the community, which puts its social hospitable walls about us from the day of our birth till we are cradled again, in our coffin, and the sides of the pit are sweet to our crumbling flesh.

We remember before thee the ages that are past and gone, and thank thee for the great men whom thou causedst to spring up in those days, great flowers of humanity, whose seeds have been scattered broadcast along the world, making the solitary place into a garden and the wilderness to blossom like a rose. We bless thee for the great men who founded the state, and for the inventors of useful things, large-minded men who thought out true ideas, and skilful-handed folk who made their lofty thought an exceeding useful thing. We thank thee for those strong men of science in whose hands the ark of truth has been borne ever onward from age to age, for poets and philosophers whose deep vision beheld the truth when other men perceived it not, and for those gifted women whose presentient soul ran before the mighty prophet's thoughtful eye, forefeeling light when yet the very East was dark with night. Yea, we thank thee for the goodly fellowship of all these prophets of glory, the glorious company of such apostles, and the noble army of martyrs, who were faithful even unto death.

Chiefliest of all do we bless thee for that noble son of thine, born of a peasant mother and a peasant sire, who in days of great darkness went before men, his life a pillar of fire leading them unto marvellous light and peace and beauty. We thank thee for his words, so lustrous with truth, for his life, fragrant all through with piety and benevolence; yea, Lord, we bless thee for the death which sinful hands nailed into his lacerated flesh, where through the wounds the spirit escaped triumphant unto thee, and could not be holden of mortal death. We thank thee for the triumphs which attend that name of Jesus, for the dear blessedness which his life has bestowed upon us, smoothing the pathway of toil, softening the pillow of distress, and brightening the way whereon truth comes down from thee, and life to thee goes ever ascending up. Father, we thank thee for the blessings which this great noble soul has widely scattered throughout the world, and most of all for this, that his spark of fire has revealed to us thine own divinity enlivening this mortal human clod, and prophesying such noble future of achievement here on earth and in thine own kingdom of heaven with thee.

Father, we thank thee also for the unmentioned martyrs, for the glorious company of prophets whom history makes no written record of, but whose words and whose lives are garnered up in the great life of humanity.

O Lord we bless thee for all these, and, in our own day, when thou hast given us so many talents and the opportunity so glorious for their use, we pray thee that we may distinguish between the doctrines of men and thine eternal commandments, and that no reverence for the old may blind our eyes to evils that have come down from other days, and no fondness for new things ever lead us to grasp the hidden evil when we take the specious good; but may we separate between the right and the wrong, and choose those things that are wise to direct, and profitable for our daily use. O Lord, when we compare our own poor lives with the ideal germ which warms in our innermost soul, longing to be itself a strong and flame-like flower, we are ashamed that our lives are no better, and we pray thee that in time present and in all time to come we may summon up the vigor of our spirit, and strive to live lives of such greatness and nobleness that we shall bless our children and all who come after us, giving them better institutions than ourselves have received, and bequeathing to them a more glorious character than was transmitted to us. May we cultivate every noble faculty of our nature, giving to every limb of the body its proper place and enjoyment, and over all the humbler faculties may we enthrone the great commanding powers, which shall rule and regulate our life into order and strength and beauty, and fill our souls with the manifold delight of those who know thee and serve thee and love thee with all their understanding and all their heart.

In the stern duties which are before us, Father in heaven, may thy light burn clear in our tabernacle, and when thou callest us may our lamps be trimmed and burning, our loins girt about, our feet ready sandaled for the road, and our souls prepared for thee. Thus may thy kingdom come, and thy will be done on earth as it is in heaven.

X.

JANUARY 11, 1857.

O THOU Infinite Spirit, who art present where *two or three are gathered together,* and who with all thine infinite perfections encampest about each solitary soul, we would draw near unto thee, who art never far from any one of us, and in thy presence gird up our souls and worship thee with such communion and income of spirit in our morning prayer that we shall serve thee all our life, bearing with patience our daily cross, and reverently doing with strength the duties thou givest us to do. May we worship thee who art Spirit, with our spirit and the truth of every faculty; and wilt thou, who seekest such to worship thee, accept the psalm of our lips and the aspiring of our heart.

O Thou Infinite One, we thank thee for the winter with which thou hast overcast the world, for we know that in every flake of snow thou sheddest from the heavens thou hast a benediction writ for all mankind, could our eyes but read the lustrous prophecy so curiously announced.

We thank thee that thou givest to mankind, in our

body and in our soul, the power over these material things that are about us. We thank thee that in the midst of the winter's snow we can build us our pleasant habitation, and have a perennial summer all safe from winter's desolating frost. We thank thee for the large power thou hast given us to make even the storms serve the voyage of our life, and to use the very ice of Northern realms as the servant of man's pleasure and the handmaid of his health. Father, we bless thee for the wondrous faculties which thou hast treasured up within the frame of man.

We bless thee for all periods in our life. We thank thee for the infancy, which is from thine own kingdom of heaven, cradled in love on earth, the little flower prophetic of other love that is to come, given not less than received, in the never-ending progress of the immortal soul. We thank thee for the period of the young man's and the young woman's life, when the body, unwonted to the experience of the world, runs over with the vernal energies of life's incipient year. We thank thee for the energy of passion, and the power of soul which thou givest us to tame this creature into wise and virtuous strength. We bless thee for the high hopes, the generous aspirations, and the quick and mounting instincts of the soul, which belong to the young man's life. We bless thee for the hardier vigor of the middle-aged, whom experience has made more wise, and we thank thee that frequent stumbling bids us take heed to our ways, and by many a failure and fall mankind is warned of the difficulties that beset his path. We thank thee for the mighty power of will that can restrain passion in its instinctive swing, and hold ambition from its wicked aim, which else might mar and desolate the soul. We thank thee for the yet later period, when thou crownest the experienced head with silver hairs without, and within hivest up the manifold treasures of long-continued life. Father, we thank thee for the instinctive power of the young, the sober calculating strength of the middle-aged, and the long-treasured glories of old men, found in the paths of righteousness, whose head is a lamp of white fire carried before us to warn us of the wrong, and to guide thy children to ever-increasing heights of human excellence.

O Lord, we pray thee that we may all of us use so nobly the nature thou hast given us, that in early, or in middle, or in advanced life, there may be such a strength of pious trust in thee as shall give thy children the victory in the day of their youth, and they may overcome the passions which else would war against the soul; and, in the middle way of mortal life, may it abate the excessive zeal of ambitious selfishness, and bring down all covetousness and every proud thing that unduly exalts itself against thee; and in the later days of mankind, may it be a strong staff in the old man's hand, and a lamp full of heavenly fire which goes before his experienced feet, guiding him still farther forward, still higher upward, and leading to serene and blameless abodes of beauty and of oneness with thee.

O Thou Infinite One, we thank thee for the opportunities of our daily life. And for its trials, shall we not thank thee? If in our feebleness we dare not thank thee for the crosses that are laid on us and the disappointments which vex our mortal affections, still, O Lord, we will bow our faces before thee, and with thankful hearts exclaim, The Lord giveth, let Him take away when he will.

Father, we pray thee that we may live so generous and aspire so high that our noblest prayer shall be the practice of our daily life, and so by continual ascension we shall rise up towards thee, enriched from thy fulness of joy, and the gladness and peace which thou givest, with no miracle, to every earnest and aspiring child of thine. So may thy kingdom come and thy will be done on earth as it is in heaven.

XI.

JANUARY 18, 1857.

O THOU Infinite Presence, who art close to each of us, we would draw near to thee, and lift up our souls unto thee, who art to be worshipped in spirit and in truth. O Lord, whither shall we flee from thy spirit, or whither shall we go from thy presence? In the beauty of summer thou wert with us, and out of genial skies sent down thy sweet beatitude of loving-kindness and tender mercy, and in the midst of winter thou art with us still, in the ground under our feet and the heavens above our head, and thine exceeding precious providence tempers even the austerity of the season for the world's great wants.

Father, we thank thee for all the periods of our earthly life. We bless thee that we are born of thy kingdom of heaven and come into this world, darting before us the prophetic rays of noble growth in times that are to come. Yea, we thank thee that from this morning dawn of infancy there goes out so fair and glorious a light, adorning the little home, and shedding its splendor far up the sky, leading the parental vision farther and farther on. We bless thee for the young men and women, and the middle-aged, for their stalwart strength of body and mind, their vigorous hope, and their power to do, to be, and to suffer, and to grow greater and greater. We thank thee for the duties which thou givest thy children to do, and the strength with which thou girdest their loins, and the power with which thou anointest their heads. We remember before thee the venerable face and the hoary hairs, which thou givest as the crown of life to those who pass on in the journey of time, doing its duties, bearing its cross, and tasting its cup of joy and of grief. We thank thee for the strong beauty of venerable age when it is found in the way of righteousness, and the firm and manly form goes before mankind, with the light of righteousness shining white and beauteous from the aged head.

O Lord, we thank thee for the blessed light of immortality which thou sheddest down on all the periods of human life, shining in its morning freshness on the baby's cradle, tending in its meridian march the progress of the grown man, and for the evening brilliancy, the many-colored rays of hope and beauty, wherewith it silvers the countenance of the old man. O Lord, when thou takest to thyself, out of the midst of us, the young, the middle-aged, or those venerable with accumulated time and manifold righteousness, we thank thee that we know they but rest from their labors, and their good works, gathered up in their character, follow them, and shine with them as a raiment of glory in the kingdom of heaven, brightening and brightening forever and forever, unto still more perfect day.

O Lord, we thank thee for our fathers who brought us up, who have gone before us and blessed us with manifold kindness and tenderness; and we bless thee also for the mothers who bore and carefully tended us, and watched over our little heads, and trained our infantile feet to walk in the ways of pleasantness and in the paths of peace.

We thank thee for the noble nature which thou hast given to woman, for the various faculties wherein she differs from man, for her transcendent mind which anticipates his slower thought. We bless thee for her generous instincts of morality, of loving-kindness and tender mercy, and that deep religious power of intuition whereby she communes with thy spirit face to face, and knows thee and loves thee with an exceeding depth of noble heart. We thank thee for the great and lustrous women of other times and our own age, who spoke as they were moved by thy spirit, or who, with lives more eloquent than speech, ran before the world's great prophets and redeemers, smoothing the pathway which rougher feet were yet to tread, and shedding the balsam of their benediction on the air which mankind was to breathe. We bless thee for the noble and generous women in our own day, engaged in the various callings and lots of human life. We thank thee for those who relieve the sick, who recall the wandering from the way of wickedness, who smooth the pillow of suffering, who teach and instruct those that are ignorant, who lift up such as are fallen down, and overtake the aged or the juvenile wanderers who are outcasts from the world. Father, we thank thee for all these blessings which thou givest to the world in this portion of humanity.

We bless thee for those noble and generous emotions which thou hast placed within the soul of man, for the continual progress which they are making, and the certainty of their triumph at last over all malice and wrath and hate and everything which makes war on the earth. We thank thee for the far-reaching love that goes out towards those who need the assistance of our arm, and for that feeling, stronger than the earthly interests of the body, which leads us to forgive every wrong which our brothers trespass against us.

We bless thee for the religious faculty which thou hast placed here within us, that in our darkness it gives us something of morning light, and, when other things fail and pass away, it breaks through the clouds, and looks up to thine own kingdom of eternal peace, and there finds comfort and rest for the soul. O Lord, we thank thee that thereby thou art to us exceeding near, strengthening us in our weakness, enlightening in our ignorance, warning in temptation; and, when we go stooping and feeble, our faces bowed down with sorrow, we thank thee that in the midst of this outer darkness, in our heart it is all full of glorious light, and thy presence is there, and thy peace is spread abroad on the afflicted and mourning one.

Father, when thou gatherest to thyself those who are of our earthly family, changing their countenance and taking them away from our arms, if we are not strong enough to thank thee for all the angels which descend and come into our house and bear away thence those whom our hearts most tenderly do love, still we thank thee that we know it is thine angel which comes, and thou sendest him here on an errand of mercy, and we thank thee that our soul can follow along the luminous track which the fiery chariot of Death has left behind, and our eye can rest on the spiritual form now clothed with immortality, and dearer to us still than when on earth. We thank thee that through all the clouds of grief and sorrow thy holy ghost comes down with quickening influence, bringing healing on his wings, and shedding abroad the glorious sacrament of consolation on eyes that weep, and stealing into the most secret heart that mourns.

Father, we remember before thee those who are needy, who in this inclement season of the year are pinched with cold, whom hunger looks sternly in the face, and we pray thee that our own hearts may be opened to do good and to communicate to those who need our service, and whom our alms-giving may doubly bless.

Help us, O Thou Infinite Father, to use the nature

thou hast given us wisely and well. We would not ask thee to change thy law, the same yesterday, to-day, and forever, but pray that ourselves may accord our dispositions to thine own infinite excellence, and order the outgoings and incomings of our heart in such wisdom that our lives shall continually be in accordance with thy life, that thy will shall be the law of our spirits, and thy love prevail forever in our hearts. So may we be adorned and strengthened with manifold righteousness, mount up with wings as eagles, run and not be weary, or walk and never faint. So may thy kingdom come, and thy will be done on earth as it is in heaven.

XII.

FEBRUARY 22, 1857.

O THOU Infinite Spirit, who thyself art perpetual presentness, whom heaven and the heaven of heavens cannot contain, but who hast thy dwelling-place in every little flower that blooms, and in every humble heart, — we would draw near unto thee, and worship in thy presence, with such lifting up of our heart and our soul that all our daily lives may be a continual service before thee, and all our days thy days. We know that thou needest not to be worshipped, nor askest our prayer's poor homage at our lips; but, conscious of our dependence on thee, feeling our weakness and our ignorance, and remembering the blessings with which thou fillest our cup, we flee unto thee, and would pour forth the psalm of our morning prayer, that we may be strengthened and blessed by the great religious emotions which raise us up to thee.

Father, we thank thee for the exceeding beauty of this wintry day, we bless thee for the ever-welcome countenance of the sun, so sweetly looking down upon our Northern land, and bidding Winter flee. We thank thee for the moon which scarfs with loveliness the retreating shoulders of the night, and for all the wondrous majesty of stars wherewith thou hast spangled the raiment of darkness, giving beauty to the world when the sun withdraws his light.

Father, we thank thee for all thy precious providence which rules over the summer and the winter, the spring and the autumn, beautifying this various and fourfold year. We thank thee that thy spirit is with us even in the darkness, which is no darkness with thee, but under thy care we can lay us down and sleep in safety, — thou giving to thy beloved even in our sleep — and when we awake we are still with thee.

We thank thee for the great land in which we live; we bless thee for its favored situation, and its wide spread from ocean to ocean, from lake to gulf. We thank thee for the millions of people who have grown up here in the midst of the continent. We bless thee for all the good institutions which are established here; we thank thee for whatsoever of justice is made into law of the state, for all of piety, of loving-kindness and tender mercy which are taught in many a various church, and practised by noble women and earnest men.

We bless thee for our fathers, who in their day of small things put their confidence in thee, and went from one kingdom to another people, few and strangers there, and at last, guided by a religious star, came to this land, and put up their prayers in a wilderness. We thank thee that the desert place has become a garden, and the wild forest, full of beasts and prowling men, is tenanted now with cities and beautiful with towns. We bless thee for the great men whom thou gavest us at every period of our nation's story; we thank thee for such as were wise in council, those also who were valiant in fight, and by whose right arm our redemption was wrought out. We thank thee for those noblest men and women who were filled with justice, with benevolence and with piety, and who sought to make thy constitution of the universe the common law of all mankind. We bless thee for those whose names have gone abroad among the nations of the earth to encourage men in righteousness and to turn many from the evil of their ways.

We thank thee for the unbounded wealth which has been gathered from our fields, or drawn from the sea, or digged from the bosom of the earth, and wrought out in our manifold places of toil throughout the land. We bless thee for the schools which let light in on many a dark and barren place; and we thank thee for noble and generous men and women in our own day who speak as they are moved by thy holy spirit, and turn many unto righteousness.

But we mourn over the wickedness that is still so common in our land; we lament at the folly and the sin of those in high place, and the others who seek high place; we lament that they tread thy people down, and bear a false witness in the land. We thank thee that the world's exiles find here a shelter and a home, with none to molest nor make them afraid; but we mourn also that the world's saddest exiles are still our own persecuted and afflicted and smitten. We remember before thee the millions of men whose hands are chained that they may not lift them up, and whose intellect and conscience the wicked statutes of men still keep in Egyptian night. O Lord, we pray thee that we may suffer for all the wickedness that we commit, till we learn to turn off from the evil of our ways, and execute thy commandments, and follow after the righteousness which thou hast written in our heart. We pray thee that thou wilt chastise us in our property and in our lives, till we learn to put away from the midst of us the yoke of bondage, and to smite no longer with the fist of wickedness.

We remember before thee our own private lives, the joys thou givest us, our daily bread and our nightly sleep, the strength of our bodies, so wonderfully made, and the vigor and hope of our intellect, conquering the world; yea, we thank thee for the affections which join us together, and the soul which unites us to thee. We remember before thee the duties thou givest us to do, and we will not ask thee to do our work, wherefor thou hast given us sufficient strength; but we pray thee that with manly and womanly might we may exercise the faculties thou hast given us, and do our work whilst it is yet called day. May there be in us such a reverence for thy being and those qualities which are thyself, that every day we shall serve thee with blameless fidelity, and grow constantly in grace, attaining nearer and nearer to the measure of the stature of a perfect man. When we turn from thy ways, and, bleeding, come back again, may we be taught thereby to wander no more from the paths of righteousness, but ever to journey in those ways which are pleasantness and lead to peace. So may thy kingdom come and thy will be done on earth as it is in heaven.

XIII.

MARCH 15, 1857.

O THOU Infinite Power, whom men call by varying names, but whose grandeur and whose love no name expresses and no words can tell; O Thou Creative Cause of all, Conserving Providence to each, we flee unto thee, and would seek for a moment to be conscious of the sunlight of thy presence, that we may lift up our souls unto thee, and fill ourselves with exceeding comfort and surpassing strength. We know that thou wilt draw near unto us when we also draw near unto thee. Father, we thank thee that while heaven and the heaven of heavens cannot contain thine all-transcendent being, yet thou livest and movest and workest in all things that are, causing, guiding and blessing all and each.

We thank thee for the lovely day which thou pourest down on the expecting world, giving the hills and the valleys a foretaste of the spring that is to come. We thank thee for the glories thou revealest to the world in darkness, where star after star travels in its far course, or to the human eye is ever fixed, and all of these speak continually of thy wisdom and thy glory, and shine by thy love's exceeding, never-ending light.

We bless thee for the love which thou bearest to all the creatures which thou hast made. We thank thee that we know that thou art our Father and our Mother, and tenderly watchest over us in manifold and secret ways, bringing good out of evil, and better thence again, leading forward thy child from babyhood to manhood, and the human race from its wild estate to far transcending nobleness of soul.

Father, we thank thee for the vast progress which mankind has made in the ages that are behind us. We bless thee that truth is stronger than error, and justice breaks down every throne of unrighteousness, and the gentleness of love is far stronger than all the energy of wrath, and so from age to age gains the victory over the savage instincts of wild men.

We thank thee for the great men and women whom thou in all times hast raised up, the guides and teachers unto humbler-gifted men. We thank thee for the philosophers who have taught us truth, and for the great poets who have touched man's heart with the fire of heaven and stirred to noble deeps the human soul. We bless thee for those expounders of thy law whose conscience has revealed thine ever live ideas of justice, and who have taught them to men. We bless thee for those warm-hearted champions of mankind whose arms of philanthropy clasp whole nations to their heart, warmed with the noble personal life of such. Yea, we thank thee for those of great religious sense, who have taught mankind truer ideas of thee, and wisely guided the souls of men, thereby controlling passion and leading thy children in paths of pleasantness and of peace. We thank thee that in no land hast thou ever left thyself without a witness, and while material nature proclaims thy glory, and day unto day uttereth speech, and night unto night showeth forth thy praise, that our human nature still more largely proclaims thy greatness and thy goodness, and the presence of thy providence, watching over all. We thank thee for the goodly fellowship of prophets in all lands, and called by many names; for the glorious company of apostles, speaking in every tongue, and the noble army of martyrs, whose blood, reddening the soil of the whole world, has made it fertile for noble human purposes.

And, while we thank thee for these, we bless thee also for the unrecorded millions of men of common faculties, who were the human soil whereon these trees of human genius stood, and grew their leaves so shady and so green, and their fruit so sound and fair. O Lord, we thank thee for the humble toiling millions of men who earnestly looked for the light, and finding walked therein, passing upward and onward towards thy kingdom, blessed by thee.

We thank thee for all the triumphs which mankind has achieved, by the few of genius or the many who have had faithful and earnest souls. We thank thee for all of truth that is demonstrated in science, for all of beauty that is writ in poetry or stamped on the rock by art. We bless thee for what of justice is recorded in books, or embodied in institutions and laws. We thank thee for that philanthropy which begins to bless the world, and here in our own land achieves such noble works. And we thank thee for what we know of true religion, of the piety that warms the innermost heart, and the morality which keeps the laws which thou hast writ.

We bless thee that in this land all men are free to worship thee as they will, or to close their eyes and look not at thine image, no human scourge laid on their earnest flesh. Father, we thank thee for the great religious ideas which have sprung down from heaven in our own day, unknown to ancient times, and for the light which they shed along the path of duty, in the way even of transgression, and for the glorious hope which they enkindle everywhere.

And while we thank thee for these things, we pray thee that we may walk faithful to the nature thou hast given us and the light which has dawned down from heaven all around. Father, we thank thee for the power of gratitude which thou givest to thy children, for the joy which men take in favors received from the highest or the humblest of the earth, and the far exceeding delight which comes to our soul from the consciousness of receiving blessings from thyself, who givest to mankind so liberally and upbraidest not, nor askest ever for our gratitude, but still art kind even to unthankful and to wicked men.

Father, we bless thee for such as love us and those whom we love in the varying forms of affection, thanking thee for the sacramental cup of joy in which thou givest the wine of life to all of thy children, humble or high.

Father, when we suffer in our hearts, when our houses are hung with blackness, and the shadow of death falls on the empty seat of those dear and once near to us, we know that there is mercy in all that thou sendest, and through the darkness we behold thy light, and thank thee for the lilies of Solomon that spring out of the ground which Death has burned over with his blackness and sprinkled with the ashes of our sorrow.

We remember before thee the various temptations with which we are tried, praying thee that in the hour of passion the youth may be strong and find himself a way of escape from its seductive witchery; and in the cold and more dangerous hour of ambition, when the maturer flesh so often goes astray, we pray thee that we may turn off from covetousness, from desire of power and vainglory amongst men, and keep our souls clean and undefiled in the midst of a world where sin and wickedness walk in the broad day. Father, within our soul may there be such an earnest and strong love of the qualities of thy being that we shall keep every law which thou hast writ on our sense or in our soul, and do justly and love mercy and walk manfully with thee, doing our duty with nobleness of endeavor, and bearing such cross as time and chance, happening to all, may lay on us. So may thy kingdom come and thy will be done on earth as it is in heaven.

XIV.

MAY 24, 1857.

O THOU Perpetual Presence, whom our hearts constrain us to bow down before, and delightedly to look up to, we would draw near to thee once more, secluding our spirits for a moment from all the noises of the world, and continue the psalm of our thanksgiving by aspirations of the soul that are higher and higher yet. We know that thou rememberest us, nor needest thou the music of our psalm nor the faint warbling of our prayer to stir thy fatherly and motherly heart to bestow upon us thy tender mercy and thy loving-kindness. Yea, we know that when earthly father and mother forget us and let us fall, thou takest us up, and in thy right hand bearest thy children forward; nay, when in the wickedness of our heart or the frailty of our flesh we break thy laws and would hide our faces from thee, thou still revealest thyself in justice and in love, and in secret ways overtakest us, liftest us up when we have fallen, and leadest us from our errors and our sins.

O Thou Infinite One, we thank thee for the fairness and the beauty which thou pourest down from the heavens above our head. We bless thee for the genial warmth which goes abroad in the air this day from the golden shining of the sun. We thank thee for the footsteps of Spring throughout our Northern land, giving new vigor to the cattle's grass, and causing hope to spring up with the farmer's slow-ascending corn. We thank thee for the promise of the season, silent or musical, in all the tenants of the sky, and for the prophecy which begins to blossom from many a tree, foretelling the glories of summer, and the appointed weeks of harvest, which are yet to come. We thank thee for the ground under our feet, the great foodful earth, and the heavens above our head, and for the whole universe of worlds which thou hast created, and sustainest with thy presence, filling all things with life, and enchanting the whole with order and beauty and love. We thank thee that by ways which as yet we know not, thou bringest many things to pass, and makest all this globe of lands, and these heavens, and the secret forces which are hid everywhere in ocean, land, and sky, to serve the great purposes of humankind. We thank thee for the meaning that is concealed in every stone, or which flames out in the flowers of the field or the stars of heaven, teaching wisdom to all of thy thoughtful daughters and thy sons.

Father, we thank thee for the revelation which this outward world of nature makes of thyself, that above us and about us there is continually thy presence, which shines in the stars of night, and moves in the wind by day, and grows in the grass, and all things doth pervade. We thank thee that thy providence watches over all, the world of matter and the world of conscious life; that thou orderest all of our movements, and from the beginning understandest the well-prepared end, making all things work together for thy final purpose of eternal good.

We thank thee for the noble nature which thou hast given unto man, making us the master over things underneath our feet and above our head, and placing the elements in subjection to us all around.

We thank thee for the triumph of truth over error, to us so slow, to thyself so sure. We bless thee for every word of truth which has been spoken the wide world through, for all of right which human consciences have perceived and made into institutions.

We thank thee for that love which setteth the solitary in families at the beginning, and then reaches wide arms all around, and will not stay its hold till it joins all nations and kindreds and tongues and people into one great family of love. We bless thee for the noble men and women whose generous heart has lit the altar fire of philanthropy in many a dark and else benighted place.

We thank thee for the unbidden faith which springs up in our hearts, impelling us to trust thee and love thee and keep every commandment of thine, and that while we know not what a day shall bring forth, we are sure of everlasting life, and while our own strength is so often weakness, we know that the almightiness of thy wisdom, thy power, thy justice and thy love, is on every living creature's side, and thou wilt bless every child of thine infinite affection. Father, we thank thee for the silent progress of the true religion, that everywhere throughout the world thou hast those that worship thee, —

> "Even that in savage bosoms
> There are longings, yearnings, strivings
> For the good they comprehend not,
> And the feeble hands and helpless,
> Groping blindly in the darkness,
> Touch thy right hand in that darkness,
> And are lifted up and strengthened."

Father, we bless thee for the discipline of our daily life, and pray that by our experience we may grow wiser and nobler-hearted, that prosperity may teach us to be generous towards all, to be charitable towards such as we ought to help; and when sadness and adversity come over us, may they still more soften our hearts, while they confirm and strengthen our will, and lift our souls upward to an aspiration for nobler and nobler virtues than we have hitherto attained. In the midst of our sadness, when crosses are laid on us that are hard to bear, and the bitter cup of disappointment is offered to our lips and it may not pass away, Oh, may our soul be so strong that with a valiant might we shall submit us to thee, and grow stronger and richer even by our sorrow and our loss, and come forth triumphant at last, with the crown of righteousness on our brows, and the certainty of acceptance with thee in our soul. Then, when thou hast completed thine earthly work with us, wilt thou take us to thyself to be with thee forever and ever, brightening and brightening towards the more perfect glory, as thou leadest us by thy spirit. So may thy kingdom come, and thy will be done on earth as it is in heaven.

XV.

MAY 31, 1857.

O THOU Infinite One, who dwellest not only in temples made with hands, but art a perpetual presence, living and moving and having thy being in every star that flowers above and every flower that flames beneath, we flee unto thee, who art always with us, and pray that we may commune with thy spirit face to face for a moment, feeling thy presence with us, and pouring out our gratitude unto thee; and amid all the noises of earth, may the still small voice of thy spirit come into our soul, wakening our noblest faculties to new life, and causing the wings of the spirit to grow out on our mortal flesh. O Thou Infinite One, we lift our thoughts unto thee, our dependent souls constraining us unto thee, that we may rest us under the shadow of thy wings, and be warmed by thy love, and sheltered and blessed by the motherly tender mercy wherewith thou regardest all of thy children. We adore and worship thee, calling thee by every name of power, of wisdom, of beauty, and of love; but we know that none of these can fully describe thee to ourselves, for thou transcendest our utmost thought of thee, even as the heavens transcend a single drop of dew which glitters in their many-colored light.

We remember before thee the manifold works of thy hand, and thy providence which hedges us in on every side. We thank thee for the genial warmth which is spread abroad along the sky, we bless thee for the green grass growing for the cattle, and the new harvest of promise just springing from the sod, foretelling bread for men in months to come. Father, we thank thee for the flowers, those later prophets of Spring, which on all the New England hills now utter their fragrant foretelling of the harvest which one day shall hang from the boughs, and glitter and drop and enrich the ground.

O Lord, we thank thee for the nation within whose borders the lines of our lot have been cast. We thank thee for our fathers, men of mighty faith, who came here and planted themselves in the wilderness, few in numbers and strangers in it, and yet not weak of heart, and lifting up valiant hands before thee. We thank thee for what truth they brought, what truth they learned, and all the noble heritage which is fallen to our hands.

We bless thee for every good institution in the midst of us, for schools and churches, for the unbounded opportunity here in these Northern States to develop the freedom of our limbs, and enjoy the liberty of our souls, wherewith thou makest all men free.

We remember before thee our daily lives, and we

thank thee for the bread we eat, the garments we put on, and the houses which more loosely clothe us, sheltering from the summer's heat or the winter's cold.

We bless thee for the dear ones who garment us about, sheltering us more tenderly and nearly. We bless thee for those who love us, and whom with answering love, we love back again; those under the sight of our eye, or lifting up their prayer with us, and those far severed from the touch of our hand or the hearing of our voice. We thank thee for these blessed relationships which set the solitary in families, making twain one, and thence manifold, beautifying the world with all the tender ties which join lover and beloved, husband and wife, parent and child, and with kindred blood and kindred soul joining many children, grown or growing, into one great family of love.

Father, we thank thee for the great ideas of our own nature, and the revelation and inspiration which thou makest therein; for the grand knowledge of thyself, our Father and our Mother, full of infinite perfection, doing good to each greatest and each smallest thing, and making all things work together for the good of each. O Lord, we thank thee for the knowledge which comes from the inspiration of thy spirit working in the human soul, and human souls obedient thereunto working with thee.

We remember our own daily lives before thee, and we mourn that, gifted with a nature so large and surrounded with opportunities so admirable, we have yet often stained our bodies with our soul's transgression, and that unclean and unholy sentiments have lodged within us, yea, nestled there and been cherished and brooded over by our consciousness. We lament that we have had within us feelings which we would not that others should bear towards us, and have done unrighteous deeds. We take shame to ourselves for these things, and we pray thee that we may gather suffering thence and sorrow of heart, till we learn to cast these evils behind us, and live nobler and more natural lives, inward of piety, and outward of goodness towards all.

We remember our daily duties before thee, the hard toil which thou givest us in our manifold and various avocations, and we pray thee that there may be in us such a confidence in our nature, such earnest obedience to thee, we reverencing all thy qualities and keeping thy commands, that we shall serve thee every day, making all our life one great act of holiness unto thee. May our continuous industry be so squared by the golden rule that it shall nicely fit with the interests of all with whom we have to do, and so by our handicraft all mankind shall be blessed. We remember the temptations that are before us, when passion from within is allied with opportunity from without, and that we have so often therein gone astray; and we pray thee that the spirit of religion may be so strong within us that it shall enable us to overcome evil and prove ourselves stronger from every trial.

We remember the sorrows and the disappointments

we must bear, and we pray that this same spirit of religion may lift us up when we are bowed down, and strengthen us when we are weak, and give joy of heart to our inner man when the mortal flesh weeps and our eyes run down with tears. Yea, may we then be conscious of immortal life, and, lifting up holy hearts, enjoy that kingdom of heaven which is not meat and drink, and here on earth, by the various steps of joy and sorrow, may we mount up to that high dwelling-place where we taste those joys which the heart hath not conceived of, but which thy spirit and our own spirit create for every earnest and noble and aspiring soul.

O Lord, we remember before thee our country, and while we thank thee for the noble fathers and mothers who here planted this national vine, and bless thee for the truth those men brought, and the justice which secures for us the liberty of our flesh and the freedom of our soul, — we remember also the wickedness in high places, in our Northern lands and in many a Southern State, which is throned over the necks of the people. We remember the millions of our brother-men whose chained hands cannot this day be lifted up to thee, whose minds are dark with the ignorance we have forced upon them, and whose souls are in bondage because we have fettered their feet and manacled their hands. O Lord, we pray thee that the whole nation may suffer till the Church and State be ashamed of their wickedness, and the whole people rise in their majesty and cast out this iniquity from the midst of us, and righteousness covers the land as the waters cover the sea. And we pray thee that in our humble way we may be useful in these great and good works, that our daily lives may be a gospel unto men, and the brave words that we speak and the noble sentiments that we cherish may be a prophecy of better things to come, which shall ring in the ears of the nation till they tingle and its heart also be touched. So may thy kingdom come, and thy will be done on earth, as it is in heaven.

XVI.

JUNE 14, 1857.

O THOU Spirit who art everywhere, and watchest over us in darkness and in light, we flee unto thee, and for a moment would mingle our spirits with thine, remembering our weakness, and also our strength, rejoicing gratefully in the good things thou hast given us, and lifting up manly aspirations towards thee, who every joint supplieth and quickeneth our soul, and seeking consciously to attain to a greater excellence than we have yet achieved here on earth. We would spread out our lives before thee, remembering our trials, our transgressions, our joys, and our sorrows, and any little triumph which we may have gained; and from these things we would gather up the materials to light our sacrifice, that its flame may go up before thee, incense from the altars of earnest hearts. May the spirit of prayer guide us in our devotions, that we may be quickened by the dew of thine inspiration and warmed by the daylight of thy providence, so that we may bloom into beauty and bear fruit to perfection in our mortal life.

We thank thee for thine infinite care and the providence which thou exercisest over every great and every little thing; for thine higher law which rules the ground underneath our feet, and whereby the most ancient heavens are fresh and strong. O Lord, thou hast numbered the hairs of our head, and not a sparrow falleth to the ground save by thine infinite providence, blessing the hairs which thou hast numbered, and caring for the sparrow in its fall.

Our Father, we thank thee for the world thou hast placed us in. We bless thee for the heavens over our head, burning all night with such various fire, and all day pouring down their glad effulgence on the ground. We thank thee for the scarf of green beauty with which thou mantlest the shoulders of the temperate world, and for all the hopes that there are in this foodful earth, and for the rich promise of the season about us on every side.

We thank thee still more for the nature which thou hast given us, for these earthen houses of the flesh wherein we dwell, and for this atom of spirit, a particle from thine own flame of eternity which thou hast lodged in the clay.

We thank thee for the large inheritance which has come down to us from other times. We bless thee that other men labored, and whilst thou rewarded them for their toil, that we also have entered into the fruit of their labors, and gather where we have not strewed, and eat where we toiled not.

We thank thee for the noble institutions which other days have bequeathed unto us. We thank thee for those great and godly men, speaking in every tongue, inspired by thy spirit, whom thou raisedst up from age to age, bearing witness of the nobleness of man's nature, and the nearness of thy love towards all the sons and daughters of men, — their life a continual flower of piety on the earth, drawing men's eyes by its beauty, and stirring men's souls by the sweet fragrance of its heavenly flame.

Most chiefly would we thank thee for him who in an age of darkness came and brought such marvellous light to the eyes of men. We thank thee for the truths that he taught, and the glorious humanity that he lived, blessing thee that he was the truth from thee, that he showed us the life that is in thee, and himself travelled before us the way which leads to the loftiest achievements.

We thank thee for those whose great courage in times past broke the oppressor's rod and let the oppressed go free. And we bless thee for the millions of common men, following the guidance of their leaders, faithful to their spirit, and so to thee, who went onward in this great human march, in whose bloody footsteps we gather the white flowers of peace, and lift up our thankful hands to thee.

Father we thank thee for the men and women of great steadfastness of soul in our own times not less, who bear faithful witness against iniquity, who light the torch of truth and pass it from hand to hand, and sow the world with seeds whence in due time the white flowers of peace shall also spring. We thank thee that thy spirit is not holden, but that thou pourest it out liberally on all who lift up earnest hearts unto thee. We thank thee for the great truths which are old, and the new truths also which are great, and for the light of justice, for the glories of philanthropy, which human eyes have for the first time in this age beheld. O Lord, we thank thee that the glories which kings and prophets waited for have come down to us, and thou hast revealed unto babes and sucklings those truths which other ages yearned for and found not.

O Thou who art Father and Mother to the civilized man and the savage, who with equal tenderness lookest down on thy sinner and thy saint, having no child of perdition in thy mighty human family, we remember before thee our several lives, thanking thee for the joys that gladden us, the work which our hands find to do, the joy of its conclusion, and the education of its process.

We are conscious of our follies, our transgressions, our stumblings by the way-side, and our wanderings from the paths of pleasantness and peace. We know how often our hands have wrought iniquity, and ourselves have been mean and cowardly of heart, not daring to do the right which our own souls told us of; and we pray thee that we may suffer from these things, till, greatly ashamed thereof, we turn off from them and live glorious and noble lives.

We thank thee, O Father, for those who make music about our fireside, whose countenance is a benediction on our daily bread, fairer to us than the flowers of earth or the stars of heaven. We thank thee for those newly born into this world, bringing the fragrance of heaven in the infant's breath; and if we dare not thank thee when our dear ones are born out of this world, and are clothed with immortality, yet we thank thee that the eye of our faith can follow them still to that land where all tears are wiped from every eye, and the only change is from glory to glory.

We thank thee for the joy and satisfaction which we have attained to in our knowledge of thee, that we are sure of thy perfection, and need not fear anything which man can do unto us. Yea, we thank thee that, through red seas of peril, and over sandy wastes of temptation where no water is, the pious soul still goes before us, a light in the darkness, a pillar of cloud by day, to guide us to the rock that is higher than we, and to place our feet in a large place, where there are fulness of joy and pleasures for evermore.

O Thou who art infinite in thy power, thy wisdom, and thy love, — who art the God of the Christian, the Heathen, and the Jew, blessing all mankind which thou hast made to inhabit the whole earth, — we thank thee for all thy blessings, and pray that, mindful of our nature and thy nearness to us, we may learn to live to the full height of the faculties which thou hast given us, cultivating them with such large and generous education that we shall know the truth and it shall make us free, that we may distinguish between these ever-living commandments of thine and the traditions of men, that we may know what is right and follow it day by day and continually, that we may enlarge still more the affections that are in us, and travel in our pilgrimage from those near at hand to those needing our help far off, and so do good to all mankind, and that there may be in us such religious trust that all our daily work shall be one great act of service and as sacramental as our prayer. Thus may we be strengthened in the inner man, able at all times to acquit us as good soldiers in the warfare of life, to run and not be weary, to walk and never faint, and to pass from glory to glory till we are transfigured at last into the perfect image of thy spirit. Then, when thou hast finished thy work with us on earth, when the clods of the valley are sweet to our weary frame, may our soul go home to thee, and so may we spend eternity in the progressive welfare which thou appointest for thy children. And here on earth may the gleams of that future glory come upon us in our mortal life, clearing up the difficult paths and strengthening our heart when it is weak within us. So may thy kingdom come and thy will be done on earth as it is in heaven.

XVII.

JUNE 28, 1857.

O THOU Infinite Spirit, who occupiest all space, who guidest all motion, thyself unchanged, and art the life of all that lives, we flee unto thee, in whom we also live and move and have our being, and would reverence thee with what is highest and holiest in our soul. We know that thou art not to be worshipped as though thou neededst aught, or askedst the psalm of praise from our lips, or our heart's poor prayer. O Lord, the ground under our feet, and the seas which whelm it round, the air which holds them both, and the heavens sparkling with many a fire, — these are a whisper of the psalm of praise which creation sends forth to thee, and we know that thou askest no homage of bended knee, nor heart bowed down, nor heart uplifted unto thee. But in our feebleness and our darkness, dependent on thee for all things, we lift up our eyes unto thee; as a little child to the father and mother who guide him by their hands, so do our eyes look up to thy countenance, O Thou who art our Father and our Mother too, and bless thee for all thy gifts. We look to the infinity of thy perfection with awe-touched heart, and we adore the sublimity which we cannot comprehend. We bow down before thee, and would renew our sense of gratitude and quicken still more our certainty of trust, till we feel thee a presence close to our heart, and are so strong in the heavenly confidence that nothing earthly can disturb us or make us fear.

Father, we thank thee for this beautiful day which thou hast given us, for the glory which walks over our heads through the sky, for the pleasing alternation of light and shade, and all the gorgeous beauty wherewith thou clothest the Summer in her strength, making her lovely to the eyes of men. Father, we thank thee that thou never failest to thy world, but sheddest dew on meadows newly mown, and rainest down thine inspiration from the clouds of heaven on every little grass and every mighty tree. Father, we thank thee that thou feedest and carest for all thy creatures, the motes that people the sunbeams, and the sparrows which fall not to the ground but by thy providence, protecting with thy hand the wandering birds of summer, and the wandering stars of heaven, holding them all in the golden leash of thy love, and blessing everything which thou hast made.

O Thou Infinite One, we thank thee for thy precious providence, which is new every morning and fresh every evening and at noonday never fails. O Thou whom no name can tell, whom all our thoughts cannot fully comprehend, we rejoice in all thy goodness; we thank thee that from seeming evil thou still educest good, and better thence again, and better still, in thine own infinite progression, leading forward and upward every creature which thou hast made.

We thank thee for our body, this handful of dust so curiously and wonderfully framed together. We bless thee for this sparkle of thy fire that we call our soul, which enchants the dust into thoughtful human life, and blesses us with so rich a gift. We thank thee for the varied powers thou hast given us here on earth. We bless thee for the far-reaching mind, which puts all things underneath our feet, rides on the winds and the waters, and tames the lightning into useful service. We thank thee for the use and the beauty which our thoughtful minds create, the grass of use for humble needs, the bread of beauty for loftier and more aspiring powers. We thank thee for this conscience, whereby face to face we commune with thine everlasting justice. We thank thee for the strength of will which can overpower the weakness of mortal flesh, face danger and endure hardship, and in all things acquit us like men.

O Thou who art the King of Love, we thank thee for these genial affections which knit us to our kind. We bless thee for the love which sets the solitary in families, which makes one of twain, and thence many more, born from love, and growing up to kindred love again. We thank thee for the kindly sentiment which brings to pass the sweet societies of friendship, of kinsfolk and acquaintance, the joy of neighborhoods, the wide companionship of nations; and for that philanthropy, which, transcending the narrow bounds of individual life, of family, kinship, neighborhood, and nation, goes round the world, looking for the ignorant to teach them, for the needy to fill them with bread, and for the oppressed to set them free.

O Thou Infinite One, who hast poured out treasures more golden yet, we thank thee for this religious sense, whereby we know thee, and, amid a world of things that perish, lay fast hold on thyself, who alone art steadfast, without beginning of days or end of years, forever and forever still the same. We thank thee that amid all the darkness of time, amid joys that deceive us and pleasures that cheat, amid the transgressions we commit, we can still lift up our hands to thee, and draw near thee with our heart, and thou blessest us still with more than a father's or a mother's never-ending love.

O Lord, we thank thee for these bodies, we bless thee for this overmastering soul, which only quits the flesh to dwell with thee in greater and more glorified magnificence forever and forever. We thank thee for those of past times or our own day who have brought to human consciousness the greatness of our nature, the nearness of thy presence, and the certainty of thy love. We bless thee for those whose words have taught, whose living breath still teaches us wiser desires, simpler manners, grander truths and loftier hopes, and chiefliest of all for those whose lives reveal to us so much that is human that we clap our hands and call it divine.

Our Father, we pray thee that we may use the blessings thou hast given us, and never once abuse them. We would keep our bodies enchanted still with handsome life, wisely would we cultivate the intellect which thou hast throned therein, and we would so live with conscience active and will so strong that we shall fix our eye on the right, and, amid all the distress and trouble, the good report and the evil, of our mortal life, steer straightway there, and bate no jot of human heart or hope. We pray thee that we may cultivate still more these kindly hearts of ours, and faithfully perform our duty to friend and acquaintance, to lover and beloved, to wife and child, to neighbor and nation, and to all mankind. May we feel our brotherhood to the whole human race, remembering that nought human is strange to our flesh but is kindred to our soul. Our Father, we pray that we may grow continually in true piety, bringing down everything which would unduly exalt itself, and lifting up what is lowly within us, till, though our outward man perish, yet our inward man shall be renewed day by day, and within us all shall be fair and beautiful to thee, and without us our daily lives useful, our whole consciousness blameless in thy sight. When new blessings are born to us in the body, when kindred souls are born out from the body to the kingdom of heaven, may we accept thy varying dispensation, which on the one hand gives and on the other takes away, and still triumphantly exclaim, It is thy hand, O God! Yea, so may we live on earth that our daily toil shall renew a right spirit within us, that the temptations of business shall open the eye of our conscience that we may see justice and conform our will thereto, and our heart grow warmer and wider every day, and our confidence in thee so firm and absolute that it cannot change and will not be afraid. Father, help us to know thee as thou art, to understand thee as thou revealest thyself in this world that is about us, as thou hast spoken through mightiest men in other days, and still more to read that older as that newest Scripture ever written on our soul, that we may know thee in thine infinity, perfect in thy completeness, and complete in thy perfections. And whilst we know thee and love thee, may we overcome every fear of chance or change, every fear of disaster and storm and fate. Thus may thy kingdom come, and so thy will be done on earth as it is in heaven.

XVIII.

JULY 5, 1857.

OUR Father who art in heaven, and on earth, and everywhere, who dwellest not only in houses made with hands, but hast thy dwelling-place wherever a human heart lifts up a prayer to thee, we would flee unto thee, and, gathering up our spirits from the cares and the joys and the sorrows of life, would commune with thee for a moment, that so we may be made stronger for every duty and more beautiful in thy sight. May thy holy spirit rest upon us, and pray with us in our morning prayer, teaching us what things we should ask, and how to pray thee as we ought.

O Thou who art everywhere, and fillest all the world, we thank thee for the freshness and beauty of this summer's day. We thank thee for the fair broad world wherein thou castest the lines of our earthly lot, for the sky above us, burning all night with starry fire, for the splendor which gladdens the gates of morning and of evening, and the beauty which by day possesses the heavens with its serene presence, adorning the figure of every cloud. We thank thee for the ground under our feet, for the green luxuriance that is spread on all the hills and fields, for the rich harvest now yielding to the mower's scythe, to be swept into his crowded barns; and that other harvest, a wave-offering of bread for man, or which hangs abundant, growing or ripening, from many a tree all round the land. For these things we bless thee, remembering it is thou who fulfillest the wants of every living thing, opening thy hand and satisfying thy children with needed bread. We bless thee likewise for the beauty which unasked for springs up by the way-side, and broiders every human path, or which thou givest us the power to produce from out the cold hard ground. We thank thee for the lilies and the roses which grow obedient to the gardener's thoughtful call, beautifying the fields and adorning many a house; and bless thee for thy loving-kindness which scatters wild roses along every rural path and about the margin of many a pond, and on the borders of every sluggish stream plants thy lilies, wherewith the enamored water, pausing in the beauty of its course, wantons, as it were, upon its handsome shores. O Thou Infinite One, we thank thee that thou revealest thyself not only in books writ with human pens, but in all the stars above, in every blade of grass, in every fruit and flower which the gardener's thoughtful care produces from the ground, or in these, the roses and lilies which thy beneficent hand profusely scatters by many a pond and long-lingering stream.

We remember before thee our own lives, and thank thee for these bodies so hopefully and wonderfully made, and these over-mastering souls which enchant a handful of dust into living, thinking, and worshipping frames of matter, that are so animated with heavenly life. We bless thee for our daily work which feeds and clothes our bodies, and, though we ask it not, which instructs our understanding, and elevates our earnest conscience and heart and soul.

We remember before thee those that are near and dear to us, bone of our bone, and flesh of our flesh, whose very presence is a joy, and whose recollection is a blessing to our heart. O Lord, we remember before thee those whose flesh the grave hides from our eyes, but who are still life of our life, soul of our soul, those who have ceased from their labors and have gone home to thy more intimate presence, rejoicing, and advancing from glory to glory.

We remember before thee the trials thou givest us, and the temptations, often too strong for us to bear, and we pray thee that we may rouse up every noblest faculty in us, and so live that though our outward man should perish, the inward man may be renewed day by day, advancing towards the measure of the stature of a perfect man. O Father who art in heaven, O Mother who art near us always, we pray thee that there may be such religious faithfulness in us that not only the prayer of our Sunday morning shall be acceptable to thee, but all the work of our daily life be blameless and beautiful, holy as a sacrament, and a continual service unto thee. May there be such confidence in thee, such love of thee, and such fidelity towards thee, that we shall bring down every high thing which exalts itself, and make every member of our body and every faculty of our soul to serve thee in our joy, and serve thee in our toil, and even in our sorrow and our sighing to serve thee not the less.

Our Father, who art of purer eyes than to behold iniquity, who blessest all of thy children, we remember before thee the great country in which thou hast cast the lines of our lot. We thank thee for the broad land thou hast given us, the mighty seas which are tributary to our thought; we bless thee for the vast multitude of people, and the great riches which our hands have won from the soil under our feet, from the waters that are round us, from the air that is over our head, and the mines which are hid in the bosom of the ground.

We remember before thee the days of our small things, and we thank thee for those pilgrims who were moved with such greatness of piety that they refused to obey the wickedness of men. We thank thee that thou sustained them when they went from their own land, that thou wert with them in all their perils, and didst bring them out of deep waters and plantedst their feet here in a large place. We thank thee for the vine which here our fathers planted where they hewed the wilderness away; .we bless thee that they tended it with their prayers, and watered it with their tears, and defended it also with their blood. We thank thee for those patriots who drew the sword in the day of extreme need, who put to flight the armies of the aliens, through whose wounds we are healed, and whose blows, smote by their right hand, have wrought for us our political redemption. Father, we thank thee for the women whose valiant eyes looked on and encouraged the hardier flesh of father, brother, husband, lover, or son.

And now, Lord, we bless thee for the fair institutions which they founded here. We thank thee for what of freedom we enjoy in the state, for all of education which comes from wide-spread schools, for the instruction which the unbridled press furnishes for all. We thank thee for what of justice is made law, for all of right which has become the common custom of the people, for the happiness which has ensued to us all.

But, Lord, with shame and weeping, we lament the sins which thy people have committed against thee; that, with all the blessings of other days gathered in our arms, with all the strength of holy institutions and of great ideas enlarging our consciousness, we are still a people so proud and so wicked, who tread thy law underneath unholy feet. Father, we mourn that we have trodden the needy down to the ground, that we have broken the poor to fragments and ground them to the dust, and on the day of the nation's jubilee we mourn that the hands of millions of men are chained together, and their minds are fettered by ignorance. Yea, Lord, we take shame and confusion of face to ourselves that we suffer this monstrous sin to linger in the midst of us, making the nation's face gather blackness in its walk on earth. We mourn that our rulers are base, and the prayer of the people has become an abomination before thee, because of our wickedness and the oppression with which we have tortured the weakest of men. We will not ask thee to save us in our sins, to free us from the consequence of wrong, while we fold the evil in our mistaken arms, but we pray thee that we may be afflicted in our basket and store, that our great men may be vanity, and our governors a lie, till we repent of our wickedness and put away the evil from the midst of us.

O Thou Infinite One, who hast given us strength proportioned to our need, we pray that we may use the faculties thou hast given us to overcome the evil that lies before us in our path. May our minds devise the right way, our conscience point to us the justice which we should follow, and our hands work out our own redemption, even as thou commandest in every bone of our body and every faculty of our soul. So may we serve our nation better even than our fathers, the patriots or the pilgrims, being faithful to the light of our day and generation, and walking whither thou wouldst have us to go. So may light come forth, and beauty and holiness cover the whole land, and peace and joy and righteousness be the possession of us all. Thus may thy kingdom come and thy will be done on earth as it is in heaven.

XIX.

NOVEMBER 1, 1857.

OUR Father who art in heaven, and on earth, we thank thee that in houses made with hands, and everywhere, thou revealest thyself to thy children, and we flee unto thee with our psalm of thanksgiving and our words of prayer, to bless thee for all that thou givest, and to quicken our souls in heavenly aspiration, that while thou drawest near unto us we may draw near unto thee, and in thee live and move and have our being. May the words of our mouths and the meditations of our hearts be acceptable in thy sight, O Lord, our Strength and our Redeemer.

We thank thee for all the blessings thou givest us, for the ground beneath our feet, and the heavens over our head, for the sun which gently parts the morning clouds, and from his golden urn pours down the handsome day all round our northern land, and for the million eyes of heaven which all night look down upon a slumbering world, full of thine own wisdom, and radiating thy love, which never slumbers and doth not sleep. We thank thee that thy spirit, which animates nature with its overflowing currents, fills also the heart and soul of man.

We thank thee for all the good which thou doest to us, for thy loving-kindness and thy tender mercy, which are over all thy works. We thank thee that thou takest care of oxen, and hast thine own thought for every great and every little thing which thine hands have made. We bless thee that we can both lay us down and sleep in safety, and when we wake that we are still with thee. We thank thee for thine infinite knowledge and thy power, wherewith thou createdst the all of things, foreseeing the end before the beginning yet was, and making all things work together for the good of all and each. We thank thee that we know that thou holdest the universe like a violet plant in thine hand, warmest it into life with thy breath, and inspirest it with thine own beauty, and blessest it with thyself. We thank thee that thou watchest over the course of human affairs, and bringest good out of evil, light out of darkness, and continually leadest forward thy children, step by step, from the low state wherein thou wert pleased to create mankind, to higher and higher heights of nobleness, as thou developest thy children to youth, to manhood, yea, to the measure of the stature of a complete and perfect man. We thank thee that thou hast nowhere left thyself without a witness, but everywhere makest revelations of thyself, where day unto day uttereth speech of thee, and night unto night showeth knowledge; yea, where there is no other voice nor language, thou, Lord, speakest in thine infinite wisdom and thy boundless love. We thank thee for the presence of thy holy spirit everywhere, that thou persuasively knockest at every closed heart, and into open souls comest like the sweetness of morning, spreading there the delight of truth and piety, and loving-kindness and tender mercy too.

We thank thee that while we are sure of thy protecting care, thy causal providence, which foresees all things, we can bear the sorrows of this world, and do its duties, and endure its manifold and heavy cross. We thank thee that when distress comes upon us, and our mortal schemes vanish into thin air, we know there is something solid which we can lay hold of, and not be frustrate in our hopes. Yea, we thank thee that when death breaks asunder the slender thread of life whereon our family jewels are strung, and the precious stones of our affection fall from our arms or neck, we know thou takest them and elsewhere givest them a heavenly setting, wherein they shine before the light of thy presence as morning stars, brightening and brightening to more perfect glory, as they are transfigured by thine own almighty power.

We thank thee for all the truth which the stream of time has brought to us from many a land and every age. We thank thee for the noble examples of human nature which thou hast raised up, that in times of darkness there are wise men, in times of doubt there are firm men, and in every peril there stand up heroes of the soul to teach us feebler men our duty, and to lead all of thy children to trust in thee. Father, we thank thee that the seed of righteousness is never lost, but through many a deluge is carried safe, to make the wilderness to bloom and blossom with beauty ever fragrant and ever new, and the desert bear corn for men and sustain the souls of the feeble when they faint.

We thank thee for that noblest ornament and fairest revelation of the nature of man whom thou didst once send on the earth to seek and to save that which was lost. We thank thee that he withstood the sin and iniquity of his time, that he was the friend of publicans and sinners, that he broke the yoke of the oppressor and let the oppressed go free. We thank thee that he respected not the position of men, but was a friend to all the friendless, and the blessing of those ready to perish fell on his head. Father, we thank thee that he lifted up that which was fallen down, and bound that which was bruised, and was a father to the fatherless, and the savior of us all. Yea, Lord, we thank thee for his temptations and his agonies, for his trials and his bloody cross, and for all his perils so manfully borne, and the crown of human homage and divine reverence which thou didst set on his head, defiled once by a crown of thorns. And while we thank thee for these things, O Lord, we pray that the same human nature may be active in our heart, and a like heroism bear fruit in our daily lives.

Father, we thank thee for every good institution of the church which has brought life and loving-kindness unto men. We thank thee for the great saints and martyrs whose names are household words in the world's mouth, and also for those unnumbered and unnamed, who with common talents have done great service for mankind, whose holy life thou hast blessed for all the world. We remember these before thee, and thank thee for the prayers, and the toils, the tears, the blood, and the manly and womanly endeavor, whereby the wilderness has been made to blossom as the rose, and the great victories of humankind have been achieved for us.

O Thou who art our Father, and our Mother not the less, we remember these things, and we pour out our hearts in psalm of gratitude and ascending prayer of thanksgiving unto thee. We remember our own lives, the lines of our lot cast in this pleasant land, and we pray thee that we may faithfully do every duty which the age demands of us. Inheriting so much from times past, quickened by the inspiration of great men, and, still more, feeling thee a presence not to be put by, ever near to our heart, — we pray thee that there may be such religiousness of soul within us that we shall make every day a Lord's day, and all our work a great sacrament of communion with thy spirit. We pray thee that we may lay aside every weight, and forsake the sins which do most easily beset us, and run the race that is before us, pressing forward to the glorious prize which thou appointest for thy children. So may thy kingdom come and thy will be done on earth as it is in heaven.

XX.

JANUARY 10, 1858.

O THOU Infinite Perfection, who art the soul of all things that are, we would lift up our spirits and gather up our hearts, and feel thy presence, and have thee as an abiding light in our tabernacle. We would thank thee for all the blessings thou givest us, and thy precious providence whereby we live. We know that thou needest no prayer of ours to stir thee to do us good, but in the midst of things changing and passing away, our heart and our soul cry out for thee, the ever living and true God. In the moment of our adoration, while we worship thee by our prayer, may we so strengthen ourselves that we shall serve thee all our lives, by a daily work which is full of obedience to thee and trust in thy perfection.

We thank thee for the world of matter whereon we live, wherewith our hands are occupied, and whereby our bodies are builded up and filled with food and furnished with all things needful to enjoy. We thank thee for the calmness of Night, which folds thy children in her arms, and rockest them into peaceful sleep, and when we wake we thank thee that we are still with thee. We bless thee for the heavens over our head, arched with loveliness, and starred with beauty, speaking ever in the poetry of nature the psalm of life which the spheres chant before thee to every listening soul.

We thank thee for this greater and nobler world of spirit wherein we live, whereof we are, whereby we are strengthened, upheld and blessed. We thank thee for the wondrous powers which thou hast given to man, that thou hast created him for so great an estate, that thou hast enriched him with such noble faculties of mind and conscience and heart and soul, capable of such continual increase of growth and income of inspiration from thyself. We thank thee for the wise mind, for the just conscience, for the loving heart, and the soul which knows thee as thou art, and enters into communion with thy spirit, rejoicing in its blessing from day to day.

We thank thee for noble men whom thou hast raised up in all time, for the great minds who bring thy truth to human consciousness, and thereby make mankind free. We thank thee for good men who do justly, and love mercy, and walk humbly with thee, visiting the fatherless and the widows in their affliction, and keeping themselves unspotted from the world, which they feed and bless with occasional charity and ever continuous toil and thought. O Lord, we thank thee for those who love thee with all their understanding and their heart, and, loving thee thus, love also their neighbors as themselves; who overtake those that wander from the way of truth, who lift up the fallen, who are eyes to the blind, and feet to the lame, and strength and salvation to such as are ready to perish.

We thank thee that while we are brothers and sisters to each other, thou art Father and Mother to us all, and when earthly parents forsake and let us fall, when our own kinsfolk and acquaintance turn from us, thou wilt hold us up and in nowise let us fall.

We remember before thee our daily lives, the duties thou givest us to be done, and we pray thee that we may have manly and womanly strength to do whatsoever our duty requires, and to bear any cross that is laid upon us, how hard and grievous soever to be borne. We remember before thee the joys thou givest us, and we pray thee that while our own heart is filled with gratitude to thee for the blessings which our hands have wrought, or have fallen as an inheritance to our lot, we may run over with loving-kindness and tender mercy to our fellow-men.

O Lord, we remember the sorrows with which thou triest us, which make our eyes run down with tears, and we pray thee that there may be in us such serenity of trust in thy providence that every tear shall be changed to a far-prospecting glass, whereby distant glories shall be brought near, and things seemingly small shine out in their real grandeur before our eyes, and ourselves be comforted even by the affliction thou givest us, and grow strong by what else would weaken heart and soul.

We pray thee that there may be in us a pure and blameless piety, which, knowing thee in thine infinite perfection, loves thee with all our understanding and our heart and our soul; and so loving thee, may we keep every law which thou writest on our material bodies, or in our spiritual soul, and live blameless and beautiful in thy sight, doing the duties of time, yet conscious of eternity, and so in a little time fulfilling a great time, and journeying ever forward and upward, till we are transformed into that perfect image of thyself, when thy truth is our thought, thy justice is our will, and thy love is the law of our daily life, as we go from glory to glory. So lead us forward through the varying good and ill of this life, and, at last, when we have finished our course on earth, and the clods of the valley are sweet to our perishing flesh, then wilt thou clothe us with the garments of immortality, and take us to thyself, ever in an ascending march to go higher and higher in those glories which eye hath not seen, nor ear heard, nor the heart of man conceived of in its highest golden dream. So may thy kingdom come and thy will be done on earth as it is in heaven.

XXI.

JANUARY 31, 1858.

OUR Father who art in heaven, and on earth, and everywhere, we know that thou rememberest us, for we stand forever before thy throne, and thou needest not the psalm of our lips nor our heart's ascending prayer to stir thy love towards us, but sometimes in our weakness do we dream that thou needest to be entreated, and so ask thee to draw nigh to us; but we know it is for us to draw near to thee, who art ever present with us, about us, and above us and within. O Thou Perpetual Presence, we thank thee for thy loving-kindness and tender mercy, in the consciousness of which we would spread out in our memory the recollection of our daily lives, the wrong deeds we do, the joys we delight in, the duties that are hard to be done, and the high hopes that kindle heaven within our heart; and while we muse on these things for a moment, we would so adore and worship thee in our prayer that we may serve thee always in our daily life.

Father, we thank thee for the material world which thou hast placed all around us, underneath, and overhead. We thank thee for the sun, which across the wintry land pours out the beauty of the golden day, checkering the year with exceeding loveliness. We thank thee for the night, visited with troops of stars, and for the moon which walks in brightness from the East to the West, gladdening the eyes of wakeful men. We thank thee for the wondrous use there is in this material world, which feeds and shelters with house and raiment our mortal flesh, which is kind with medicines to our various ailments, and furnishes manifold tools for our toil and thought.

We thank thee for the greater world of spirit, whereof thou hast created us in thine own image and likeness, vested with immortality, having here a foretaste of everlasting life. We thank thee for our body, so curiously and wonderfully made, and for the spirit, which far transcends this vast material world. We thank thee for the mind, which loves use and beauty and truth; for this conscience which would know right, and the overmastering will which would do it all our days. We bless thee for the affections, which join us to some bright particular star, or tie us to some pleasant nook of earth; which ally us with the animals about us, and most tenderly do find their home in father and mother, in lover and beloved, husband and wife, parent and child, and all the sweet companionships which gladden our earthly loving heart. We bless thee for the feeling infinite, the religious soul which thou hast planted in us, of higher kinship than the mind, the conscience, or the earthly affections; yea, we thank thee for this soul, which without searching can find out thee, and hold communion with thee at our own sweet will, receiving blessed inspiration from thy presence, which is not to be put by.

We thank thee for the relation which thou hast established between that world of matter which is without us and this world of spirit which is within; and we thank thee that while material nature furnishes food and shelter, instruments and healing to our mortal flesh, it likewise furnishes far higher things to mind and conscience, and to heart and soul. Yea, we bless thee that thou hast made all things work together for good; that while we are striving with prayer and toil for daily bread, thou givest us also the bread of life, and feedest us with spirit's food, and so nursest us upward till we grow to the measure of the stature of a complete and perfect man. O Lord, what is man that thou art mindful of him? Thou hast created him a little lower than the angels, and hast crowned him with glory and honor and immortality, and hast put all things underneath his feet.

We remember our daily lives before thee, the wrong things which we have done, and the unholy thoughts and evil emotions which we have not only suffered in our hearts but cherished there. We pray thee that thou wilt chasten us for these things, and we may suffer and smart therefor till we turn from every wrong, and with new life efface the scars of ancient wickedness wherewith we have stained and deformed our consciousness.

We remember before thee the special blessings thou hast given, and while we would not forget thy hand, which feedeth us forever and forever, we would let our hearts, when filled with gratitude to thee, run over with their loving-kindness and tender mercy to mankind, till our hands also are filled with good deeds, whereby we hold communion with our brother-men.

We remember the stern sorrows which thou givest us, the cup of bitterness oft-time pressed to our lips, the trials which await us in our business and perplex our understanding; we remember the sorrows which stain our eyes with tears when thou changest the countenance of our dear ones, and lover and friend are put far from us, and our acquaintance into darkness. O Father in heaven, O Mother on earth and in heaven too, we thank thee that we know that it is unto brightness, and not darkness, that thou ferriest our acquaintance over, carrying our dear ones into thine own kingdom of heaven. We thank thee for the spirits of just men made perfect already, and for those whom, in infinite progression, thou leadest forward from the stain of earthly sin to that purity and perfection which the eye hath not seen, nor the ear heard, nor our human hearts but poorly, dimly felt.

Father, we thank thee that while earthly things perish and pass away, and we know not what a day shall bring forth, we are sure of thine infinite power, wisdom, justice, and love, and when our mortal decays and passes down to the sides of the pit, and the clods of the valley are sweet to our perishing frame, we thank thee that we still feel thy presence as not to be put by, and the calm still voice of thy spirit pleads with us, teaching of duty and assuring us of its infinite reward.

O Father in heaven, we will not ask thee to work a miracle and draw nigh to us, thou who art ever living in our life and moving in our motion, and yet transcending time and space. But we pray thee that there be such action of our noblest part that we shall think truth, that we shall know right and will it all our days, that we shall love things given us to love, and grow in our affection stronger and stronger to our brother men, closer and closer knit; and may there be such action of our soul that we shall know thee as thou art, and live with a perpetual income of thy spirit to ourselves, even in our sleep thou giving to thy beloved, and we receiving from our Father and our Mother, whose warmth shall make us warm, whose life is our living. Day by day may we pass from the glory of a good beginning to the greater glory of a noble end, and when at last thou hast served thyself with our mortal bodies, may we lay them in the dust, whence these garments of the soul were taken first, and clothed with immortality, fly upwards, onwards unto thee. So may thy kingdom come, thy will be done on earth as it is in heaven.

XXII.

FEBRUARY 14, 1858.

O THOU Infinite One, who art a perpetual presence above us, and about us, and within, we would draw near unto thee, who art not far from any one of us, and with a consciousness of thy presence would remember before thee all the blessings thou hast given us, the duties which we are to do, the crosses which must be borne, the joys we delight in, and the sorrows which afflict us; remembering these things, we would so worship thee for a moment that we may serve thee all the days of our lives. Our Father who art in heaven, whither shall we flee from thy presence, whither shall we go from thy spirit? If we take the wings of the morning and dwell in the uttermost parts of the sea, even there shall thy hand lead us, and thy right hand shall hold us up. We thank thee for thy loving kindness and thy tender mercy, which are over all thy ways, beneath which we can lay us down and sleep in safety, and when we awake we are still with thee.

We thank thee for the noble nature thou hast given us, for its vast powers to know truth and beauty, to find out the eternal right, to love one another with the strength of our affections, and to know thee, who art our Father and our Mother, and to cleave unto thee with an absolute trust, which knows no turning nor falling away.

O Lord, we remember before thee thine own presence in the world of matter, and in the consciousness of our own soul. We thank thee that thou speakest in this Old Testament of the world of nature, and in this New Testament of man's spirit makest yet more glorious revelations of thyself; and while there proclaiming thy power, thy law, thy wisdom, here in our hearts thou tellest ever of thy justice and thy love, thine infinite perfection which thou art. We thank thee for the great revelations thou hast made through the human sense and human soul in times past. We bless thee for the great men and women whom thou hast gifted so liberally with genius that they have become great philosophers, poets, and teachers of morality to mankind, in whose soul thine own image has been mirrored down and reflected back to men. We thank thee for the prophets and apostles who, in all lands and in every age, through the inspiration thou didst normally put on them, have been a guiding and shining light unto their brothers.

We thank thee that not only unto great men hast thou revealed thyself, but out of the mouth of babes and sucklings hast thou perfected thy praise, the little teaching the great, and the few instructing the many. We thank thee for the millions of common men and women, their names to mankind all unknown, who with great faithfulness of soul have looked upwards and found thee, and with the daily beauty of their lives have revealed thy loving-kindness and thy tender mercy to the world of men.

Above all others, do we thank thee for that great and noble man who in days of darkness and extreme peril thou raisedst up, and through his genius didst inspire with so much of truth, and justice, and philanthropy, and faith in thee. We thank thee for the words of truth which he spoke, for the sentiments of noble piety and philanthropy which came out not only in his speech, but in the daily works of his handsome life; and we bless thee that his words and the memory of his life have come down to us to kindle our hope, to stir our aspirations, and to strengthen our faith in man.

Father, we thank thee not only for all these things which are behind us, but that still to the human soul thou impartest thyself, giving truth to all who use their minds aright, revealing justice to every one, warming each faithful heart with love, and revealing thyself to whoso with honest purpose looks up and seeks after thee. We thank thee for all truth which we have learned of thee, for every emotion of pious gratitude and holy trust which has sprung up within our heart; and if we have achieved any elevation of character and done any good deeds in our lives, we thank thee, who givest to us all in our nature so liberally, and demandest of us only the duties which our strength is equal to, and which raise us to greater and greater powers of strength by the doing thereof.

We remember before thee our own daily lives, thanking thee for the reward which comes as the result of our toil. We bless thee for the friends near and dear, by whatsoever name they are called, still bone of our bone, and flesh of our flesh, or spirit of our soul. We thank thee that in our sorrows thou art an ever-present help, not far from us, but exceeding near, and the thought of thee not only confirms us for our duty, but refines us till we are able to bear the exceeding sorrows oft laid on us. We bless thee for the glorious hope which spreads out before us, for the consciousness of everlasting life which comes as the innermost fact of our inward soul. We thank thee that in a world where things deceive our expectations, we are sure of thee, and certain of thy loving-kindness and thy tender mercy, and the infinite heaven which spreads out before us.

We pray thee that there may be in us such knowledge of thee, such love and trust in thee, that all our days we shall serve thee with blameless and earnest work. May we do the duties thou givest to be done, and bear any crosses laid upon us, in such manly and womanly sort, that by toil and suffering we shall grow wiser and better every day. Help us to distinguish between the commandments of erring men and the everlasting commandments of thy law, which thy spirit writes on the world of matter and publishes in this world of spirit. Day by day may we grow wiser and juster, stronger in our righteous will, more loving in our affections, while our emotions towards thee become continually more and more beautiful, and blessed still the more.

We remember before thee all men, our brothers everywhere, and pray thee that by our truth and our lives we may do something to lift the cloud of darkness which blinds men's eyes, and to strike off the fetters which chain the mind or which manacle the limbs. So by our life may we serve thee, who art not to be worshipped as though thou neededst anything, and here on earth may we pass from glory to glory, till, when thou hast finished thy work with us below, thou layest our bodies in the dust, and clothest us with immortality, and, arrayed in that wedding-garment, takest us home to thyself, to pass from the glory of the earthly to the greater glory of the heavenly, and enter into those joys which eye hath not seen, nor ear heard, nor the heart of man can fully comprehend. So may thy kingdom come, and thy will be done on earth as it is in heaven.

XXIII.

FEBRUARY 28, 1858.

O THOU Infinite Spirit, who possessest the darkness of the night, and fillest the chambers of the day with thy glorious presence, we would draw near unto thee, and worship thee with the homage of grateful hearts, thanking thee for the favors for which thou askest not our gratitude, and communing with thy spirit face to face. In our darkness and our feebleness we turn ourselves unto thee, seeking to feel thee nearer and more intimately in our souls, and so to worship in our morning prayer that thy sunlight shall shine upon our heads, and in the light thereof we shall journey all our days, serving thee with a perfect service and a manly trust.

O Thou who givest us all things so richly to enjoy, we thank thee for the world wherein thou hast cast the lines of our lot. We bless thee for the night, where the moon walks in beauty, and star unto star proclaims thy loving-kindness and thy tender mercy, wherewith thou fillest up the world of space, and embracest not less the all of time. We thank thee for the handsome day, which this great star pours down from heaven, bringing the touch of Spring to our cold Northern lands, and waking the newly-ventured birds to their earliest vernal song. Father, we thank thee for all the beauty of the year, for the wondrous world which is under our feet, and above our heads, and round us on every side.

We thank thee for these bodies of ours, builded up from material things, so curiously and so wonderfully made; we thank thee for the power which thou givest them, and all their various weapons for toil and for defence. We thank thee for the noble soul thou hast enthroned herein, this divine spark, enchanting with its life this handful of material dust. We thank thee that thou hast created us in thine own image, and hast given us the power over these material things, over the earth under our feet, and the elements that are above us, and about us on every hand.

We thank thee for the large mind, rejoicing in use, in beauty, and in science not the less. We thank thee for the power thou givest us from this material world to build up our bodies, strong and handsome temples, wherein thy spirit dwells in the human form, incarnating itself in so many millions and millions of thy daughters and thy sons. We thank thee for these senses, through which the soul looks out upon the world, and at these various windows takes knowledge in, and learns so much of thy works, and has communion with thine infinite joy in the world of matter which thou hast made.

We thank thee for this conscience, with its power to know right, and its will to do right, and we bless thee that only thine own unchanging higher law of right can satisfy it, yearning for the first good, first perfect, and first fair. We thank thee that through this faculty we hold communion with thine everlasting righteousness, and can live by thy commandment, which is exceeding broad, and hath neither variableness nor the shadow of a turn.

We thank thee for these affections, whereby we love those about us, and knit many tender ties which join us each to each, and all to one another. We thank thee for the love which joins those that are of the same nation or community, for the kindred blood which throbs in mutual hearts. We bless thee for the affection which makes the lover and his beloved to rejoice together, giving welfare to the bridegroom and the bride, to wife and husband. We thank thee for all the sweet felicities which come from the relation of friend to friend, and parent to child, for the many joys which cluster round our heart, and shine like morning light within the humblest or the proudest home.

We thank thee that in addition to all these things thou givest us power to know thee, to trust thee and to love thee, with a faith that knows no change, save from glory to glory, as it brightens into the perfect day of piety and its serenest joy. We thank thee that amidst a world of things which are changing, we are sure of thine infinite loving-kindness and thy tender mercy, and even in darkness we can trust thee, knowing that thy fatherly and motherly arm is about us, leading us from strength to strength, ready to uphold us when we totter, and to lift us up when we fall down. O Thou Infinite One, we know no words to tell thee the deep emotions of our heart, the joys of our piety, and the holy trust we place in thee; and thou needest no words, nor askest thou the prayer or psalm of thanksgiving from our heart, for thou art behind us and before, and above us and below, and about us and within, and understandest every thought before our words express it in the ear.

We remember before thee the duties thou givest us to do, and we pray thee that with earnest faithfulness we may do them all. May we bear any cross thou layest on us which must be borne, with reverent patience, growing stronger from every affliction wherewith thou triest us. When those near and dear are severed from our side, and the shadow of death falls on the empty place of our friend, we would remember that other world, where all tears are wiped from every eye, and thy children pass from the greater glory to the greatest, as they are led in infinite progression by thy hand.

We remember the joys thou givest us, and while we taste them, we pray that our hearts may be filled with bounty towards all, and we may do good according to the measure of the strength which thou givest us.

We remember our daily lives, and pray thee that by bearing what must be borne, and doing what thou givest us to do, we may build ourselves up to higher and higher heights of human excellence. May we grow wiser and more just, be filled with more loving-kindness to our brother men, and have a heartier and a holier love and trust in thee. May no success in this world's affairs ever harden our heart, but make us more noble and more generous, and may the world's sorrow and sickness and grief and disappointment and loss only rouse up the better soul that is in us, till we triumph over affliction, and have gained the victory over death. Thus in our souls may there be such a bud of piety as shall open and bloom out into the fragrant flower of morality in our daily lives, and while it thus blossoms broad in use, may it bear seed within itself which shall last forever and forever. So finish thou thy work with us here below, and when it is done and ended, wilt thou take us to thyself, to be with thee forever, and so to be transfigured into higher and higher likenesses of thy spirit, and pass from glory to glory forever and ever. So may thy kingdom come and thy will be done on earth as it is in heaven.

XXIV.

MARCH 14, 1858.

O THOU Infinite One, we flee unto thee, and for a moment would be penetrated with the thought of thy presence, and so worship thee in the uplifting of our hearts that we may serve thee with our hands all the days of our mortal lives.

We thank thee for thy loving-kindness and thy tender mercy, which are new every morning and fresh every evening, and which fail not at noonday. We thank thee for the world that is about us, and above us, and beneath us, full of thy presence in every star of heaven and every flower of earth. We bless thee for the other world which ourselves are, whereto this sphere of matter is but outward resting-place and environment, and we thank thee that our souls are likewise the temple of thy spirit, and thou it is who givest us life and breath and all things richly to enjoy. We thank thee that thou hast created us from perfect love, and watchest over us with such causal providence that thou makest all things work together for good, and wilt lose no child of perdition from thy mighty human flock, but wilt lead thy children by the hand, and those who cannot walk thou wilt bear in thine arms, and bring them all at last to never-ending bliss. O Thou, who art Perfect Love, we thank thee for thyself, and, sure of thine infinite loving-kindness and thy tender mercy, we know that we cannot fail, and having thee, all else needful are we sure of beside.

We thank thee for the glorious nature which thou hast given us, that thou hast blessed us with such large faculties, to know what is useful and beautiful and true, to understand what is just and right before thine eyes; and with this affection whereby we love each other, and are joined by manifold tender ties to those who are dear to us, however far remote in time and space. We thank thee for this great and overmastering power whereby we know thee and commune with thee, thy spirit inspiring our spirit, and thy providence upholding us when we totter, and uplifting us when we fall. Father, we thank thee for all these things, and our words know not how to praise thee as our hearts so gladly would, but we know that thou needest no words from our heart, no psalm from our lips, for thou understandest us, knowing the words of our mouth before they are conceived in our heart.

We thank thee for all manner of blessings which thou givest us. We bless thee for the things needful to the body, for our health and our strength, our bread by day, our nightly sleep, and the work which our hands find to do, whereby our bodies are clothed with raiment and our mouths are satisfied with bread. We thank thee for the instruction which comes to mind and to conscience from our daily toil. We bless thee for those who are near to our heart, whether by our side or far removed, or separated even by the gates of death. We thank thee for the ascended spirits that were once with us on earth, lifting their eyes upon the sun, taking sweet counsel with us, and walking to thine house in company. We bless thee for all good and noble men and women, who from time to time come up in thy providence, to teach nations the way in which they should walk, and to call many from wickedness to the ways of justice, which lead to such blessedness on earth and beyond the world. We thank thee for ages past, for the childhood of mankind, and for any words of simplicity and truth which have come down to us from ancient days. We thank thee for the primal virtues which shine aloft as stars, and not less for the charities which heal and soothe and bless, and are scattered at man's living feet like flowers. We bless thee for the great truths which have come down to us on their sounding way through the ages, encouraging and strengthening men. We thank thee for poets and prophets and mighty men of thought and of piety, who spoke as they were moved by thine all-wakening spirit, and brought truth to mankind; and we thank thee that in our own day, not less, thy spirit still works with the children of men, O Thou, who art the head, and dost every joint supply, and art always present in the world of matter and the world of man.

We thank thee for all these things, and we pray thee that we may strengthen ourselves mightily with thy spirit in our inner man. May we turn off our eyes from loving evil things, and withhold our hand from every unclean and ungodly work. May we build ourselves up to the measure of a perfect man, growing continually to a higher image and likeness whereafter thou hast created us. May there be in us such love of thee, such faith in thee, and such obedience towards thee, that we shall keep every law thou hast written on our bodies or in our souls. Thus may we learn thy truth, and may it set us free alike from the darkness of old times and the error of our own days. May we learn what is right and do thy will, with all the strength that is in us, and while we ask thee to love us, may we love our brothers as we love ourselves, and grow constantly in the practice of every religious duty, and the doing of every manly work. Thus may thy kingdom come, and thy will be done on earth as it is in heaven.

XXV.

MARCH 21, 1858.

O THOU who art everywhere, we would feel thy presence at our heart, and lift up our spirit unto thee, seeking to hold communion with thee, and be strengthened for duties, for sorrows, and for joys. For a moment we would remember in thy presence the lives that we lead, the works thou givest us to do, our short-comings, or any success that is in us; and while we muse on these things may the fire of devotion burn within our heart and so stir us that from our moment of worship we may learn to serve thee all the days of our lives.

O Thou, who art our Father and our Mother, we thank thee for thy loving-kindness and thy tender mercy, which are over all thy works. We thank thee that thou causest thy sun to shine on the evil and on the good, and sendest thy rain on the just and on the unjust. We bless thee that with fatherly providence, with motherly love, thou carest for the enlightened people of the earth, and not less for those whom savage ignorance hath held blinded so long. We thank thee that thou lovest thy saint, and also every sinner, who is also a child of thine, and wilt suffer no son of perdition in thy great family, whom thou blessest with thyself.

We thank thee for the special providence which is over everything which thou hast created, and wherein thou residest with all thine infinite perfections. We bless thee for the rain which to-day thou sheddest out of the sweet heavens, to warm the long-chilled bosom of the ground, to swell the buds on every tree, and to waken the flowers of prophecy on all our Northern hills and in our valleys, which are full of the promise of Spring. We bless thee that, while thou givest us the earth underneath our feet and the heavens above our head, both in that which is beneath, and that which is above, and not less, O Lord, in that which is within us, thou thyself residest forever, and manifestest thyself to all the sons and daughters of men. We thank thee that in the midst of human darkness thou art an ever-glorious light, shining forever in thy beauty. We thank thee that out of seeming evil thou still educest good, and better thence again, in thine own infinite progression, and so leadest thy children ever upwards, and forward forever. We thank thee that even the wrath of man is made to serve thee, and the remainder of wrath thou dost restrain, making all things work together at last for good. We thank thee that thou carest for us all, that in our day of joy we know it is thou who fillest our cup, by giving us the faculties which make it run over at the brim. We thank thee that thou art with us in our days of hardship and of calamity, that when our own heart cries out against us, thou art greater than our heart, and, understanding all things, blessest us in secret ways; and when we are cast down, and go stooping and feeble, with hungering eyes and a failing heart, that thou still art with us, and leadest us from strength to strength, and blessest us continually.

We remember before thee the daily works wherein we are engaged, the perplexities of our business, abroad or at home, and we pray that we may have such strength of faithfulness to thee that the dark shall appear light to us, and the crooked shall become straight, and the way of duty so plain before our face that we cannot err therein.

We remember the sorrows with which we are tried, the grievous disappointments that are laid upon us; yea, we remember that thou takest from us our lover and acquaintance, those with whom we took sweet counsel, and walked to thy house in company. We remember before thee their immortality and our own, and we thank thee for the kingdom of heaven which arches over us, and sheds down its sweet influence from on high to encourage and to draw us up. And in days of sorrow we pray thee that we may have a quickening sense of this spiritual world whereto our faces are set, which is the appointed end of our earthly pilgrimage.

Father, we remember our own souls before thee; we

know how often we have been forgetful of the duty which thou demanded of us, that we have often cherished unworthy feelings, and have not felt that love to our brother men which we should have felt, or which we have asked of thee. Yea, we remember that we have stained our hands by doing wrong things, and defiled the integrity of our own consciousness, and we pray thee that we may smart for every offence which we commit against thee, till, greatly ashamed of our folly and our meanness, we pass off from the unholy ways which are evil and lead to evil, and turn to those which are pleasantness and lead to eternal blessedness beyond the grave. Father, we thank thee for any suffering which comes upon us for wrong doings, knowing that thereby thou recallest us from the evil of our ways, and would save our souls from suffering yet worse.

And we pray thee that this religious faculty may be so strongly active within us that we shall never fear thee, but a perfect love may cast out fear, and we know thee as thou art in thine infinite perfection, the Father and Mother of our soul in our every hour of need, which is our every hour of life; and may we have such love for thee, such faith towards thee, and live such a life in thee, that within us all shall be blameless and beautiful, every faculty performing its several and appointed work, and all our outward lives shall be as harmonious as the stars in their courses, and full of continual use to our brother men.

O Thou who needest not to be entreated, we do not

ask of thee new talents, for thou hast given what thou sawest fit; nor do we entreat thee to do for us what thou hast given us power to do; but, conscious of thy presence, feeling the great gifts which thou hast bestowed upon us, and the perpetual income of thy spirit, we would use every faculty which thou hast given for its appropriate work, and so pass from childhood to manhood, from glory to glory, till thou, finishing thy work with us here, shall take us to thyself, to pass from the greater glory to the greatest, by a continual transfiguration of ourselves to thine image and thy likeness. So may thy kingdom come, and thy will be done on earth as it is in heaven.

XXVI.

MARCH 28, 1858.

O THOU who art everywhere, and needest not to be entreated, nor askest the bending of our knees, nor the prayer of our lips, nor our heart's psalm unto thee, we would draw near to thee for a moment, who art always near unto us. We would remember the blessings thou givest us, the duties thou demandest, the sorrows we are tried withal, or the offences which we commit; and while we muse on these things, may the fire of gratitude and devotion be kindled on our altar, and our souls flame up towards thee, like incense from the altars of the just. From the moment of our communion with thee may we gather such strength that we shall worship thee always by a constant service from day to day.

Our Father who art in heaven, and on earth, and everywhere, we thank thee for the world of matter under our feet, and over our head, and about us on every side. We thank thee for the night which hung the curtains of darkness about us, whereunder we could lay us down and sleep in safety, and that when we awoke we were still with thee. We thank thee for the moon which walked in beauty, and checkered the darkness with her comely light, and we bless thee for the sun which from his golden urn pours day across the world, warming and blessing everything with his sweet angelic touch. We thank thee, O Lord, for the bread we eat, for the garments we put on, for the houses which hold us, for the sleep which all night slides into our bones, bringing strength to the weary, and health to the sick; and we bless thee for the day full of toil and opportunities for manly endeavor.

We thank thee for the vast gifts which thou hast bestowed upon us, for these bodies so curiously and wonderfully made, as a temple for a spirit more wondrous and far more curiously made to dwell therein awhile, enchanting the dust into wise and human life. We thank thee for the ever-questioning mind, which hungers for use and truth and beauty, wherewith thou feedest us from age to age. We bless thee for this large conscience, which seeks for justice, wherewith thou dost enlighten our eyes and quicken what is innermost within us. We thank thee for these self-denying affections, which reach out unto friends and kinsfolk, unto lover and beloved, parent and child, to countrymen yea, which spread out their arms to those that are needy everywhere. We thank thee for this religious faculty, which through the darkness looks up to thee and is filled with thy light, and we bless thee that in our hour of sorrow it brings to us exceeding tranquillity and hope and strength. We thank thee for the dear and tender joys which are born in our innermost of consciousness, which dwell there and fill the whole temple of our inner life with that presence which cannot be put by, which is a blessing to us by darkness and by day. We thank thee, Father in heaven, for all the good which has come from these great talents thou hast blessed us withal. We thank thee that in every age and every land thou givest open vision of thyself to thy children, and in the things that are seen mirrorest thine own image, O Thou whom the mortal eye cannot see, but whom our heart enfolds within itself, which is blessed by thy touch. We thank thee for great philosophers and prophets and poets, mighty men and women, whom thou hast blessed with large genius, who in many an age have gathered truth and justice, and taught love, and lived blameless piety; we thank thee for the revelations of manhood they have made to us, and the revelations of thine own spirit which through them have shone upon our heart. And for the greatest of them all, as we fondly dream, we thank thee, — for him who taught so much of truth, and lived so much of piety in his soul, and blameless benevolence in his outward life; we bless thee for his words of soberness, for his life of sacrifice and of duty, and all the gladness and joy which therefrom has come to the sons and daughters of men. We thank thee not less for the millions of unremembered souls of men and women, who in their common callings of earth were faithful to the light which shone upon them, howsoever dim; and we bless thee that by their stripes we are healed, and we also have entered into their labors, and rejoice in the heritage which their toil has won and bequeathed to us.

Remembering all these things, we would pour out our psalm of gratitude to thee, kindling a reverence and love within our heart. We remember before thee the duties thou givest us to do, and, howsoever hard, pray thee that we may stir ourselves to be equal to our task. We would not forget the sorrows that are laid upon us, the disappointments, the bereavements and afflictions, which the mortal eye of man beholds, and those dearer and worser which only thy sight sees in our heart, knowing its own bitterness; and we pray thee that we may strengthen ourselves mightily for these things, and be made wiser and better within by the sorrows which we endure, which lie patent to the world, or are hid in the recesses of our secret soul.

Of earthly things we know not how to pray thee as we ought, seeing as through a glass darkly, and not knowing whether poverty or riches, whether disaster or triumph, shall serve thy purpose best and make us noble men. But whatsoever of these things we have, whether thou gildest our pathway with the sun of sereneness, or thunderest before our face, holding the blackness of darkness over us, yet give us the noble mind which loves the truth, the conscience which though it trembles as it lowly lies looks ever to the right, the affection which makes us spend and be spent for the good of others, — give us these things, and crown these virtues with sweet loving-kindness and faith in thee which need not be ashamed.

O Thou who art our Father and our Mother, may we know thee as thou art, as thou revealest thyself in the clear depths of our soul, and knowing thee, may we love thee with all our understanding and our heart, with our strength and our soul; and making it all blameless in our inner man, may our outward life be useful also, full of beauty, and welcome in thy sight. So here on earth may we have a foretaste of thine heaven, and fly upwards towards thee, transfiguring ourselves by constant growth into thine image, till, finishing thy work with us on earth, thou layest our bodies in the grave, and to thine own home takest our spirits, to be with thee forever and forever. So may thy kingdom come, and thy will be done on earth as it is in heaven, for thine is the kingdom and the power and the glory forever and ever.

XXVII.

APRIL 18, 1858.

O THOU who art present everywhere, we know that we need not ask thee to remember us, for thou hast us in thy holy care and keeping by day and by darkness, and art the presence at our fireside and about our path, watching over our rising up and our lying down, and acquainted with all our ways. In our weakness we flee unto thee, seeking to draw near thee, to know thee as thou art, and worship thee with what is highest and best within our soul. Conscious of thy presence about us and within, and mindful of thine eye which is ever upon us, we would remember the things which make us glad, or fill us with sadness; we would think over the good deeds which beautify our soul, and the ill things which are the deformity of our spirit; and while we muse on these things, may the fire of devotion so burn in our heart that from the momentary worship of our prayer we may learn to serve thee in our daily life through all our years. May the meditation of our heart bring us nearer unto thee, and the words of our mouth carry us up and on in the great journey of our mortal life.

Father, we thank thee for this material world above us, and about us, and underneath, wherein thou hast cast the lines of our earthly lot in exceeding pleasant places. We thank thee for the stars which all night in their serene beauty speak of thee, where there is no voice nor language, yet the speech of whose silence is felt by longing, hungering and impatient souls. We thank thee for the sun, which pours out the golden day to beautify the sky, and to bring new growth of plants, and life of beast and bird, and many a creeping thing upon the ground. We thank thee for the presence of Spring with us, for this angel of growth, who weeks ago put the green oracle of the prophetic grass by every watercourse, rippling its psalm of life before the sight of men, and who now has cast his handsome garment on our plains, and whose breath swells the buds in many a vale and on many a hill, and draws the birds with their sweet music once more to our Northern land. We thank thee for the seed which the hopeful farmer casts already into the genial furrows of the ground, looking to thee, who art the God of seed-time, for the harvest's appointed weeks.

We thank thee for the human world which ourselves are; we bless thee for the large nature with which thou hast endowed us, giving us the victory over the ground and the air, making every element to serve us, and the great sun by day to measure out our time, and distant stars by night to keep watch over our place, letting us know where 'tis we stand upon thy whirling, many-peopled globe. We thank thee for the large measure of gifts, the many talents wherewith thou enrichest this soul of man, which thou createdst nobler than the beasts that perish, and giftedst with such power immense, and such immortal hope.

We thank thee for the joys of our life, our daily bread which imports strength into our bodies, the nightly sleep which brings tranquillity, recruiting us from toil past, and strengthening us for duties that spread out before.

We thank thee for the mortal friends that are around us, for the dear ones who are bone of our bone or spirit of our spirit, whom we put our arms about and fold to our heart, a gladsome sacrament to our bosom, a serene blessedness to our earthly mortal soul. We remember the new ties which join us to the world, little Messiahs born into human arms, and we thank thee for the tender ties newly knit which join the lover and his beloved, the bridegroom and the bride, and all those sweet felicities wherefor the heart, marrying itself to another, before thee pours out its natural psalm of grateful joy. We thank thee for these dear affections, whereby the earth blossoms like a rose, and far-reaching philanthropies go out to bless the distant world, counting mankind our kith and kin. We bless thee for this deep religious faculty which thou hast given us, which through the darkness of earth looks upward to thine exceeding light, the star whose sparkle never dims, but shines through every night adown upon the human soul.

We thank thee for the duties thou givest us to do, our general toil by fireside and street-side, on land or sea, or wheresoever thou sendest us to run for the prize of thine own high calling. Yea, we bless thee for trials which are not too severe for us, and for the burdens which thou layest on our manly or womanly shoulders, that for others' sake and for our own we may bear them nobly and well.

O Lord, in the light of thy countenance, how many wrong things spring up to our consciousness, and we must needs stain our prayer with some tear of penitence for an error committed, an evil deed, or some unholy emotion which we have kept within our soul. We will not ask thee to forgive us and remove from us the consequence of wrong; we know that so doing thou wouldst rob us of our right; — but we pray thee that we may learn to forgive ourselves, and with new resolution dry up every tear of penitence, and fill those footsteps which we have made in ancient error with new and manly, womanly life, bearing us farther forward in our human march.

We remember before thee the sorrows with which thou triest us, how often we stoop us at the bitter waters and fill our mouths with sadness, and if we dare not thank thee for these things, if we know not how to pray thee about them as we ought, we yet thank thee that we are sure that in all these things thou meanest us good, and out of these seeming evils still producest good, making all things work together for the highest advantage of thine every child, with whom thou hast no son of perdition and not a single castaway. We thank thee for that other, that transcendent world, beyond this globe of matter and this sphere of present human consciousness. We thank thee for that home whereinto thou gatherest the spirits of just men made perfect, and for our dear ones who have gone thither before us, and bless thee that they are still not less near because they are transfigured with immortal glory, and have passed on in the road ourselves must also tread. We thank thee for not only the hope, but the certain consciousness of immortality that is within our soul, giving us light in our darkness, hope when else we should despair; and when we are bowed down and go stooping and feeble, with failing eyes and hungering heart, we thank thee that we can lift up our countenance towards that other world, and be filled with joy and gladness of heart.

Our Father who art in heaven, we thank thee for thyself, — the materiality of material things, the spirituality of our spirit, the movingest thing in motion, the livingest of life, the all-transcending in what is transcendent. O Thou who art our Father and our Mother too, we thank thee for thy providence, which is over all thy works in this world, material, or human, or transcendent; yea, for the infinite love which thou bearest to everything which thou once hast borne.

We pray thee that we may know thee as thou art, in all thine infinite perfection of power and wisdom and justice and holiness and love, and knowing, may have within us that perfect love of thee which casts out every fear. May there be in our soul that warming strength of piety which shall give us the victory in our trial, making us strong for public or for unseen crosses that are laid upon our shoulders, and winging us with such strength that out of sorrow we shall fly towards thee, going through the valley of weeping, and coming off with not a stain upon our wings and no tear-drop in our eye. May there be in us such love of thee that we shall love every law which thou hast writ on sense or soul, and keep it in our daily lives, inward and outward, till all within us be beautiful, till our outward conduct be blameless, and we make every day thy day, all work sacrament, and our time a long communion, with use to our brothers, and with calmness, trust and love to thee. So on earth may thy kingdom come, and thy will be done here and now as it is in heaven, for thine is the kingdom and the power and the glory forever and ever.

XXVIII.

APRIL 25, 1858.

O THOU Perpetual Presence, in whom we live and move and have our being, we would draw near unto thee once more in our mortal consciousness, adoring and thanking and worshipping thee, who art of our lives our most living thing, the cause and providence of all that be. We would remember before thee the blessings thou givest to be enjoyed, the duties to be done, the crosses we bear, and the temptations we encounter; we would spread all these things out before our eyes, and look at them in the light of thy conscious presence, and while we muse thereon may the fire of devotion so burn in our hearts that from our moment of worship we may gather a continual service of thee for all time to come. So may the meditations of our hearts, and the words even of our mouths, draw us nearer unto thee, and strengthen us for duty and hope and sorrow and delight.

Our Father, who art always with us, we thank thee for the material world thou hast given us, this great foodful ground underneath our feet, this wide overarching heaven above our heads, and for the greater and lesser lights thou hast placed therein; we bless thee for the moon which measures out the night, walking in brightness her continuous round, and for the sun that pours out the happy and the blessed day all round thy many-peopled world. We thank thee for the green grass, springing in its fair prophecy, for the oracular buds that are promising glorious things in weeks to come. We thank thee for the power of vegetative and animative life which thou hast planted in this world of matter, which comes up this handsome growth of plant and tree, this noble life of fish, insect, reptile, bird, beast, and every living thing.

We thank thee for the human world whereof thou hast created us; we bless thee for the great spiritual talents wherewith thou hast endowed man, the crown of thy visible creation on the earth. We thank thee for our mind and our conscience and our heart, and all the manifold faculties which thou hast given us, whereby we put material things underneath our feet, making the ground to serve our seasons, and the sun to keep watch and distribute warmth about our garden and our farm, whereby we turn the vegetative and animative powers of earth to instruments for our bodily welfare, and our mind's and heart's continual growth.

We thank thee for the work thou givest us to do on earth, in our various callings, wide-spread in the many-peopled town, or in some lonely spot hid in the green world which compasses the town. We thank thee for all these things that our hands find to do, by fireside and field-side, in school, or shop, or house, or ship, or mart, or wheresoever thou summonest us in the manifold vocations of our mortal life.

We bless thee for the joys which we gather from our toil, for the bread which strengthens our live bodies, for the garments and houses which shield us from the world without, for all the things useful, and the things of beauty, both whereof are a joy to our spirits.

We thank thee for the dear ones thou givest us on earth, called by many a tender name of friend, acquaintance, relative, lover or beloved, wife or husband, parent or child, and all these sweet societies of loving and congenial souls. We thank thee for the joy which we take in these our dear ones, whilst they are near us on earth, and when in the course of thy providence it pleases thee to change their countenance and send them away, we thank thee still for that transcendent world whereinto thou continually gatherest those that are lost in time, and are only found in eternity, and if reft from our arms are taken to thine, O Thou Infinite Father, and Infinite Mother too. We thank thee that for all sorrows there is balm and relief, that this world which arches over our head, invisible to mortal eye, is yet but a step from us, and our dear ones, looking their last on earth, are born anew into thy kingdom of heaven, and enter into glory and joy which the eye has not seen, nor the ear heard, nor our hungering hearts ever fully dreamed of in our highest thought.

We thank thee, O Lord, for thyself, Thou Transcendent World, who embracest this material earth and this human spirit, putting thine arms around all, breathing thereon with thy spirit, and quickening all things into vegetative, animative, or human life. We thank thee that whilst here on earth, not knowing what a day may bring forth, nor certain of our mortal life for a moment, we are yet sure of thine almighty power, thine all-knowing wisdom, and thy love which knows no change, but shines on the least and the greatest, on thy saint and on thy sinner too. We thank thee for the perfect providence wherewith thou governest the world of material, of growing, or of living things; we bless thee that thine eye rests on each in all its history, that there is no son of perdition in all thy family, and that thou understandest our temptations, that thou knewest before we were born whatsoever should befall us, and that in thy fatherly loving-kindness and thy motherly tender mercy thou hast provided a balm for every wound, a comfort for every grief. We thank thee that when our kinsfolk and acquaintance pass from earth, howsoever they make shipwreck here, they land in thy kingdom of heaven, entering there in thine eternal providence, their eternal welfare made certain of before the earth began to be.

While we thank thee for these things, who needest not our thanks, while our hearts, overburdened with their gratitude, lift up our prayerful psalm unto thee, and we remember our daily duties, and the glorious destination thou hast appointed for us, we pray thee that with great and noble lives we may serve thee all the days of our mortal stay on earth. May there be in us such a pious knowledge of thee, such reverence for thee, and such trust in thee, that we shall keep every law thou hast writ on our body or in our soul, and grow wiser and better, passing from the glory of a good beginning to the glory of a noble ending, as we are led forward by thy spirit, co-working with our own. Day by day, may we proclaim our religion by our faithful industry, doing what should be done, bearing what must be borne, and at all times acquitting us like men. So may thy kingdom come, and thy will be done on earth as it is in heaven.

XXIX.

MAY 2, 1858.

O THOU Infinite Perfection, who fillest the world with thyself, and art not far from any one of us, we flee unto thee, and for a moment would draw near thee, that by the inspiration of our prayer we may know how not only to worship thee in our psalm and the adoration of our heart, but to serve thee with our work in all the daily toil of our mortal lives. We know that thou needest neither our psalm of thanksgiving, nor our aspiring prayer, but our heart and our flesh cry out for thee, the Living God, and for a moment we would join ourselves to thee, and warm and freshen our spirit in the sunlight of thy countenance, and come away clean and strengthened and made whole.

Our Father, we thank thee for the material world in which thou hast placed us. We thank thee for the return of Spring, bringing back the robin and the swallow from their wide wanderings, wherein thy providence is their constant guard, watching over and blessing these songsters of the sky. We thank thee for the buds swelling on every bough, and the grass whose healthy greenness marks the approaching summer, and the flowers, those prophets of better days that are to come. We bless thee for the air we breathe, for the light whereby we walk on the earth, for the darkness that folded us in its arms when we lay down thereunder, and that when we awoke we were still with thee. We thank thee for the bread which we feed upon, for the shelter which our hands have woven or have builded up, to fend us from annoying elements. We thank thee for all the means of use and of beauty which thou givest us in the ground and the air and the heavens, in things that move, that grow, that live. We thank thee that thou makest these all to wait on us, having kindness for our flesh, and a lesson also for our thinking soul.

We thank thee for the human world, whereof thou hast made us in thine own image and likeness. We thank thee for the great faculties which thou hast given us, of body and of mind, of conscience and of heart and soul. We thank thee for the noble destination which therein thou shadowest forth, for the great wants which thou makest in our spiritual nature, for the unbounded appetite thou givest us for the true and the beautiful, the right and the just, for the love and welfare of our brother men, and the vast and overshadowing hope which thou givest us towards thee. We thank thee for this great nature thou hast given, with its hungerings and thirstings for ultimate welfare, for duty now and blessedness to come.

We thank thee for all the various conditions of mortal life. We bless thee for the little children who are of thy kingdom, and whom thou yet sufferest to come unto us; we thank thee for these perpetual prophets of thine, whose coming foretells that progressive kingdom of righteousness which is ever at our doors, waiting to be revealed; we thank thee for the joy which these little buds of promise give to many a father's and mother's heart. We thank thee for the power of youth; we bless thee for its green promise, its glad foretelling, and its abundant hope, and its eye that looks ever upwards and ever on. We thank thee for the strength of manhood and of womanhood, into whose hands thou committest the ark of the family, the community, the nation, and the world. We thank thee for the strength of the full-grown body, for the vigor of the mature, expanded, and progressive mind, and all the vast ability which thou treasurest up in these earthen vessels of our bodies, holding for a moment the immortal soul thou confidest to their care. We bless thee for the old age which crowns man's head with silver honors, the fruit of long and experienced life, and enriches his heart with the wisdom which babyhood knew not, which youth could not comprehend, and only long-continued manhood or womanhood could mature at length and make perfect. O Lord, we thank thee that thou hast made us thus wondrously and curiously, and bindest together the ages of infancy and youth and manhood and old age, by the sweet tie of family and of social love.

We thank thee for that other, the transcendent world, which is the home of the souls thou hast disenchanted of this dusty flesh and taken to thyself, where the eye may not see, nor the ear hear, nor our own hungering and thirsting heart fully understand, all the mysterious glory which thou preparest for thy daughters and thy sons. We thank thee for the good men who have gone before us thither. We bless thee that the little ones whom thou sufferest to come unto us, when they depart from us, thou takest to this other world and watchest over and blessest there. We thank thee that thereinto thou gatherest those who pass out of earth, in their babyhood, their youth, their manhood, their old age, and settest the crown of immortality on the baby's or the old man's brow, and blessest all of thy children with thyself.

O Thou, who art Almighty Power, All-present Spirit, who art All-knowing Wisdom, and All-righteous Justice, we thank thee for Thyself, that thou art in this world of matter and this world of man, and that transcendent immortal world. Yea, we bless thee that thou art the substance of things material, the motion of all that moves, the spirituality of what is spirit, the life of all that lives, and while thou occupiest the world of matter and the world of man, yet transcendest even our transcendence, and hast thine arms around this dusty world, this spiritual sphere, and the souls of good men made perfect. We thank thee for the motherly care wherewith thou watchest over every living thing which thou hast created, guiding the swallow and the robin in their far-wandering but not neglected flight, for without thee not a sparrow falleth to the ground, and thou overrulest the seeming accident even for the sparrow's good.

Father, we remember before thee our daily lives, thanking thee for our joy, and praying thee that there may be in us such love of thee, such reverence and holy trust, that we shall use the world of matter as thou meantest us to use it all. In our daily work, may we keep our hands clean, and an undefiled heart; may we do justly, and love mercy, and walk humbly with thee. When our cup runs over with gladness, may we grow bountiful to all that need our wealth, using our strength for the weakness of other men, to lift up those that are fallen, to be eyes to the blind, and feet to the lame, and to search out the cause which we know not. We remember our sorrows before thee, and when our mortal hearts are afflicted, when sickness lays waste our strength, when riches flee off from our grasp, when our dear ones in their infancy, their youth, their manhood or old age, are lifted away from the seeing of our eyes, — may our hearts follow them to that transcendent world, and come back laden with the joy into which they have already entered. Our Father, may we so know thee as all-wise, and all just as to never fear thee, but perfect love shall cast out fear, and a continual spring-time of faith bud and leave and blossom and grow and bear fruit unto eternal righteousness. So may we pass from glory to glory, transfiguring ourselves into an ever higher and more glorious likeness of thyself, and here on earth enter into thy kingdom and taste its joy, its gladness and its peace. So may thy kingdom come and thy will be done on earth as it is in heaven.

XXX.

MAY 23, 1858.

O THOU Infinite Presence, who livest and movest and hast thy being in all things that are above us, and around us, and underneath, for a moment we would feel thee at our heart, and remember that it is in thee we also live and move and have our being. Conscious of thy presence, we would look on our daily lives, that the murmur of our business, and the roar of the streets, and the jar of the noisy world, may mingle in the prayer of our aspiration, and our devout soul may change it all into a psalm of gratitude and a hymn of ever-ascending prayer. May the meditations of our hearts and the words that issue thence draw us nearer unto thee, who art always above us and about us and within.

We bless thee for the material world, wherewith thou environest us beneath and about and overhead. We thank thee for the night, where thy moon walks in brightness, pouring out her beauty all around, with a star or two beside her; and we bless thee for the sun, who curiously prepares the chambers of the East with his beauty, and then pours out the golden day upon the waiting and expectant ground. We thank thee for the new life which comes tingling in the boughs of every great or little tree, which is green in the new-ascended grass, and transfigures itself in the flowers to greater brightness than Solomon ever put on. We thank thee for the seed which the farmer has cradled in the ground, or which thence lifts up its happy face of multitudinous prophecy, telling us of harvests that are to come. We thank thee also for the garment of prophecy with which thou girdest the forests and adornest every tree all round our Northern lands. We bless thee for the fresh life which teems in the waters that are about us, and in the little brooks which run among the hills, which warbles in the branches of the trees, and hums with new-born insects throughout the peopled land. O Lord, we thank thee for a day so sweet and fair as this, when the trees lift up their hands in a psalm of gratitude to thee, and every little flower that opens its cup and every wandering bird seem filled by thy spirit, and grateful to thee. We thank thee for all thine handwritings of revelation on the walls of the world, on the heavens above us and the ground beneath, and all the testimonies recorded there of thy presence, thy power, thy justice, and thy love.

We thank thee not less for that perpetual springtime with which thou visitest the human soul. We bless thee for the sun of righteousness which never sets, nor allows any night there, but, with healing in his beams, shakes down perennial day on eyes that open, and on hearts that, longing, lift them up to thee. We thank thee for the great truths which shine to us, the lesser light like the moon in the darkness of the night, and those great lights which pour out a continuous and never-ending day about us where'er we turn our weary mortal feet. We thank thee for the generous emotions which spring up anew in every generation of mankind, for the justice that faints not nor is weary, for the truth which never fails, for that philanthropy which goes out and brings the wanderer home, which lifts up the fallen and heals the sick, is eyes to the blind and feet to the lame; yea, we thank thee for that piety which inspired thy sons in many a distant age, in every peopled land, and we bless thee that it springs anew in our heart, drawing us unto thee, and giving us a multitudinous prophecy of glories that are yet to come, while it sheds peace along the pathway where we turn our weary mortal feet.

We remember before thee the various business of our lives, thanking thee for the bread we eat, the raiment we put on, the houses which shelter us, the tools that occupy our hands, and all this wonderful array of material things whereby thou marriest the immortal soul to this globe of lands about us and underneath. We thank thee for the process of our work, blessing thee for all which industry teaches to our intelligent hand, to our thoughtful mind, to our conscience, which would accord it with thy law, to our hearts, which would love each other, and to our soul, which gains not only daily bread for the body, but bread of life for itself, yea, angel's bread, wherewith thou administerest the industrial sacrament to our lips in our daily toil.

We remember before thee our various duties and temptations on the earth. In the time of our youthful passion, we pray thee that conscience may light its fire within our heart, to shed its light along our path, that we stumble not, nor fall into the snare of the destroyer; and in the more dangerous hour when ambition tempts the man, we pray thee that with greatness of religion we may bid this enemy also stand behind us, and wait till we bind his hands and make him bear our burdens and grind the mill whereby we achieve greater glories for ourselves. We pray thee that when we are weak and poor and foolish, we may remember the source of all strength and all riches and all wisdom; and when we grow strong and rich, wise and good, may we never forget our duty to the poor, the weak, the foolish and the wicked man, but, remembering that mercy is more than sacrifice, may we love others as we love ourselves, and forgive them as we ask thy blessing on us in our trespasses and our sins.

We remember before thee those that are near and dear to us, joined by many a pleasant tie, seen by the eyes, or felt only in the soul which trembles across distances, and with the electric bond of love joins the distant as the near. We thank thee for all that we love, and who in turn love us, and, mid the noisy world, we bless thee for the quiet satisfaction which comes to peaceful loving souls.

Father, we remember not less those who are of us, if with us no more, and while we dare not thank thee that the mortal has faded from our sight, we thank thee that we know that when friend and lover are put from us, they go not into darkness but into unspeakable light, born out of the world of time to live forever in thy glorious eternity.

Our Father, we remember before thee our whole country, thanking thee for the many blessings thou hast given us, for the great multitude of its people, for the abundance of its riches, for its industry which fails not, and its mind which grows ever the more intelligent. We thank thee for great men who in times past bore to this land the seed of promise, planted it in the wilderness, watched over it, defending with their tears, and enriching with their blood; yea, who drew swords in its manly defence. We thank thee for these men, for these great, noble, valiant souls, who in our day of pilgrimage and of revolution were faithful to mankind's sorest need, and wrought for us so great deliverance.

And now, Lord, we remember before thee one,* two years since felled by the assassin's coward hand, himself not less noble than the noblest, and by the stripes of our iniquity which were laid on him, dis-

* Charles Sumner.

abled alike from public duty and private joy, him whom the waters, cradling, rock, while he seeks in other lands the quiet and the health this cannot offer. We thank thee for his valiant soul which remembered its bravery when others thought but of discretion, and that he bore a man's testimony in the midst of an unmanly crowd of mean men, and deserved greatly of his own generation, and ages that are to come. We know that we need not ask thy blessing on him, but in our hearts we would bear his memory exceeding precious.

Father, we pray thee that in every emergency of our lives we may be faithful to the duty which the day demands, and with reverent spirits acquit us like men, doing what should be done, bearing what must be borne, and so growing greater from our toil and our sufferings, till we transfigure ourselves into noble images of humanity, which are blameless within and beautiful without, and acceptable to thy spirit. So may thy kingdom come and thy will be done on earth as it is in heaven; for thine is the kingdom and the power and the glory, the dominion and honor forever and ever.

XXXI.

JUNE 6, 1858.

O THOU Infinite Perfection, who art everywhere present, by day and night, we would flee unto thee, and for a moment take thee to our consciousness, in whom we live and move and have our being, as thou also livest and movest and hast thy being in us. Conscious of our dependence upon thee, we would remember our joys and our sorrows, praying thee that from our moment of communion and of worship we may get new strength to serve thee all the days of our lives. O Thou Infinite Mother, who art the parent of our bodies and our souls, we know that thou hast us always in thy charge and care, that thou cradlest the world beneath thine eye, which never slumbers nor sleeps, and for a moment we would be conscious of thy presence with us, that thereby we may enlighten what is dark, and raise what is low, and purify what is troubled, and confirm every virtue that is weak within us, till, blameless and beautiful, complete and perfect, we can present ourselves before thee.

Father in heaven and on earth, we thank thee for

the world of matter thou hast given us, about us, underneath us, and above our heads. We thank thee for the genial year, whose sweet breath is now diffused abroad o'er all our Northern land. We thank thee for this great inorganic and organic mass of things whereon we live. We bless thee for the world of vegetative growth which comes creeping, creeping everywhere, spreading over the shoulders of the land, and running beneath the waters of the sea. We thank thee for the flowers which adorn the green grass, and which hang their open petals in wondrous beauty yet from many a lingering tree. We thank thee for these lesser and these greater prophets who proclaim in their oracles the various gospel of the year, foretelling the harvest of grass for the cattle, and of bread for man, and satisfaction for every living thing. We thank thee for the rain thou sheddest down from heaven, abundant in its season, and the genial heat thou minglest with the air and earth, changing these seeming dead organic things to vegetative growth. We bless thee for the animated world of living things that feed upon the ground, that wing the air with their melodious beauty, or that sail unseen the depths of the sea. We thank thee for all this varied flock of speaking and of silent things which thou hast breathed upon with thy breath of life. We thank thee that from day to day thou spreadest a table for every great and every little thing, that thou feedest the fowls of heaven, and carest for the beasts of the earth, the cattle and the creeping things, taking care of oxen, and having thine eye on all the many millions of creatures which thou hidest in the waters of the sea, where thou feedest them with thy bounty, housing and clothing and healing all.

We thank thee for this great human world which thou hast superadded to this earth and air and sea. We thank thee for the mighty capacities which thou hast given us for thought and toil, for use, and beauty's sweeter use, for duty and all the manifold works of mortal time. We bless thee for the eye of conscience which thy sun of righteousness doth so irradiate with healing in his beams, and we thank thee for this blessed power of affection which makest twain one, and thence educest many forth, and joinest all in bonds of gladness and of love. We thank thee for this uplifted and uplifting soul of ours, whereby we know thee, our Father and our Mother, and have serene delight in thy continual presence and thy love.

Father, we thank thee for that transcendent world near to the earth of matter and the soul of man, wherein thou dwellest, thou and the blessed spirits thou enclosest, as the sea her multitudinous and her fruitful waves.

Father, we thank thee for thine own self, for thy fatherly loving-kindness, for thy motherly tender mercy, which are over all thy works, breaking their bread to the humbler things that are beneath us, and feeding us not less with bread from heaven, even the spiritual food which is our soul's dear sustenance. We thank thee that when we slumber and when we wake, when we think of thee, and when our minds are on the cares of earth, or the joys of friendship, thou hast us equally in thy care, brooding over us with a mother's love, sheltering us with all the perfections of thine infinite being. Yea, we thank thee that when, through the darkness that lies about us, or the grosser darkness of perverted will within, we wander from thy ways, thy motherly love forsakes us not, but thou reachest out thine arm and bringest back the wanderer, rounding home at last, a wiser and a better man, that he has sinned, and suffered, and so returned.

We remember before thee our inward and our outward lives, and pray thee that, on this material world, and of this human, and surrounded so by thee, we may live great, blameless, noble lives. May there be in us that soul of piety which so regardest thine infinite power, wisdom, justice, and love, that we shall scorn to disobey the law which thou hast writ on flesh or soul, but keep all which thou commandest, and serve thee by a life that is continually useful, beautiful, and acceptable with thee. In this spring-time of the year, half summer now, may there be a kindred spring-time in our soul, and the lesser and the greater prophets thereof, may they hang out their pleasing oracles, the gospel which promises a noble harvest of virtue in days to come. May we have such piety within, transfiguring itself to such morality without, that we shall bear every cross which should be borne, do each duty which must be done, and at all times bravely acquit us like noble men. Thus may we grow to the measure of the stature of a complete and perfect man, passing from glory to glory, till thou finishest thy work on earth through our hands, and welcomest us to thine own kingdom of heaven, to advance forever and ever, from glory to glory, from joy to joy, as we are led by thee. So may thy kingdom come and thy will be done on earth as it is in heaven.

XXXII.

JUNE 13, 1858.

O THOU who art always near to us, we in our consciousness would for a moment draw near unto thee, and, feeling thee at our heart, would remember the circumstances of our daily lives, the joys we delight in, the sorrows we bear, the sins wherewith we transgress against thee, the grave, and solemn, and joyous duties thou givest us to do.

O Thou who givest to mankind liberally, we thank thee for the world of matter wherein thou hast placed us, for the heavens above our head, for the stars that burn in perennial splendor, though the misty exhalations of the earth may hide them from our sight. We bless thee for the sun which above the clouds pours down the light, and creates a world of beauty, erelong to be opened to our mortal sense. We thank thee for this great foodful ground underneath our feet, now garmented with such loveliness, and adorned with the manifold radiance of thy loving-kindness and thy tender mercy. We thank thee for the grass everywhere growing for the cattle, and for the bread which the farmer's thoughtful toil wins by thy providence from out the fertile ground. We thank thee for the seed he has cast into its furrows, and the blade piercing the earth with its oracle of promise, foretelling the weeks of harvest which are sure to follow in their appointed time. We thank thee that in the cold rain from the skies, thou sheddest down the unseen causes of harvests both of use and of beauty which are yet to come.

We thank thee for the love with which thou givest thy benediction to everything which thou hast made. Thou pasturest thy clouds on every ocean field, thou feedest thy mountains from the breast of heaven, thou blessest the flowers on a thousand hills, thou suppliest the young lions when they hunger from lack of meat, thou clothest the lily with beauty more than queenly, and through all these outward things that perish thou speakest of thine infinite providence, which watches over every sparrow that falls, and holds in thy hand the wandering orbs of heaven.

We thank thee also for this great, glorious human nature which thou hast blessed us with. We thank thee for the body, so curiously and wonderfully made, fitted for all the various purposes of human need; and we thank thee for this spiritual part which thou hast breathed into this mortal.

We bless thee for this toilsome and far-reaching mind, which gives us dominion over the earth beneath our feet, and makes the winds and the waters serve us, which tames the lightning of heaven, and learns the time from the stars by night and the sun by day. We thank thee for that great world of artistic use and beauty, and of scientific truth, which the human mind has made to blossom from out this foodful ground and these starry heavens wherewith thou girdest us about.

We bless thee for the moral sense, hungering and thirsting after righteousness, and that thou fillest our conscience with thine own justice, enlightening our pathway with the lamp of right, shining with its ever unchanging beams, to light alike the way of thy commandments and of human toil upon the earth.

We thank thee for these dear affections, which set the solitary in families, and of twain make one, and thence bring many forth, peopling the world with infantile gladness, which grows up to manhood and to womanhood in all their various forms. We thank thee for that unselfish and self-forgetful love which toils for the needy, which is eyes for the blind, and feet for the lame, and is wisdom for the fool, and spreads civilization all round the world, giving freedom to the slave and light to those who have long sat in darkness.

We thank thee for this overmastering religious faculty, the flower of intellect and conscience and the affections, and we bless thee that by this we know thee instinctively, and have a joyous delight in thy presence, opening our flower, whereinto thou sheddest gentle dew, warming it with all thy fatherly and motherly love, blessing us from day to day, from age to age.

We thank thee for the great triumphs of the human race, that while thou createst us individually as little babies, and collectively as wild men, slowly but certainly thou leadest thy children from low beginnings, ever upward and ever forward, towards those glorious heights which our eyes have not seen nor our forefeeling hearts completely understood. We thank thee for the truth, the justice, the philanthropy and the piety, which elder ages have brought forth and sent down to us, to gladden our eyes and to delight our hearts. We thank thee for those great, noble souls whom thou createdst with genius and filledst with its normal inspiration, who have shed light along the human path in many a dark day of our human history, and in every savage land. And above all these do we thank thee for that noble brother of humanity, who, in his humble life, in a few years, revealed to us so much of justice, so much of love, and with such blameless piety looked up to thee, while he forgave his enemies, putting up a prayer for them. And not less, O Father, do we thank thee for the millions of men and women, who with common gifts and noble faithfulness have trod the way of life, doing their daily duties all unabashed by fear of men. We thank thee for what has been wrought out by these famous or these humble hands, which has come down to us.

O Lord, we thank thee for thyself, Father and Mother to the little child and the man full-grown. We thank thee that thou lovest thy savage and thy civilized, and puttest the arms of motherly kindness about thy saint and round thy sinner too. O Thou who art Infinite in power and in wisdom, we bless thee that we are sure not less of thine infinite justice and thy perfect love.

Yea, we thank thee that out of these perfections thou hast made alike the world of matter and of man, providing a glorious destination for every living thing which thou broughtest forth.

We remember before thee our daily lives, and we pray thee that in us there may be such knowledge of thy true perfection, such a feeling of our nature's nobleness, that we shall love thee with all our understanding, with all our heart and soul. We remember the various toils thou givest us, the joys we rejoice in, the sins we have often committed, and we pray thee that there may be such strength of piety within us, that it shall bring all our powers to serve thee in a perfect concord of harmonious life. In youth may no sins of passion destroy or disturb the soul, but may we use our members for their most noble work ; and in manhood's more dangerous hour may no ambition lead us astray from the true path of duty and of joy. Wherever thou castest the lines of our lot, there may we serve thee daily with a life which is a constant communion with thyself. So day by day may we transfigure ourselves into nobler images of thy spirit, walk ever in the light of thy countenance, and pass from the glory of a manly prayer to the grander glory of a manly life, upright before thee and downright before men, and so serve thee in the flesh till all our days are holy days, and every work, act and thought becomes a sacrament as uplifting as our prayer. So may thy kingdom come and thy will be done on earth as it is in heaven.

XXXIII.

JUNE 20, 1858.

O THOU Infinite Presence, who occupiest all space and all time with thy perfections, we flee unto thee, and would feel for a moment the consciousness of thee, and in the light of thy countenance would we spread out our life before thee, and so pay thee worship in our prayer that we may give thee manly and womanly service all our days, with continual cleanness of hands and gladness of heart. We know that thou needest no prayer from our lips or our hearts, but in our feebleness and dependence upon thee, we love to join ourselves for a moment, in our silent or our spoken prayer, with thee, who art our Father and our Mother, that we may gird up our loins and strengthen our spirit before thee.

O Lord, who givest to mankind liberally, and upbraidest not, we thank thee for the blessings thou bestowest from day to day. We thank thee for this material world, now clad in its garment of Northern beauty, for the great sun which all day pours down his light upon the waiting and the grateful world, and for the earth underneath our feet. We bless thee for the green luxuriance which fills up all the valleys and covers all the hills, and hangs in its leafy splendor from every tree. We bless thee for the grass, bread for the cattle, its harvest of use spread everywhere, and for the various beauty which here and there spangles all useful things which thine eye looks down upon. We thank thee for the grain which is the food of man, and for the green fruit hanging pendent on many a bough which waves in the summer wind, its wave-offering unto thee. We thank thee that all night long, when our eyes are closed, above our head there is another world of beauty, where star speaketh unto star, and though there be no voice nor language, yet thy great spirit therein watches alike over the sleeping and the wakeful world.

Father we thank thee for this great human world which thou hast created. We bless thee for the glorious nature which thou hast given us, above the material things and above the beasts who feed thereon, which thou hast made also subservient unto us. We thank thee for the vast talents, so various and so fair, which thou hast lodged in these earthen vessels of our bodies. We bless thee for our vast capacity for improvement in every noblest thing, and that thou hast so made the world that while we seek the daily bread for our body which perishes in the using, we gain also by thy sweet providence that bread of life which groweth not old, and strengthens our soul forever and ever.

We thank thee for the joys thou givest us here on earth, for the blessing which comes as the result of our daily toil, which feeds our mouths, and clothes our bodies, and houses and heals us in the world where shelter and medicine are kind to our mortal flesh. We thank thee for the education which comes from the process of all honest work, the humblest and the highest. We bless thee for the moral sense, telling us of that star of right which shines forever in thine heaven, and sheds down the light of thine unchanging law, even in the darkness of our folly and our sin. We bless thee for this great human heart by which we live, making us dear to kinsfolk and acquaintance, to friend and relation, joining the lover and beloved, wife and husband, child and parent, in sweet alliances of gentleness and love. Father, we thank thee for this soul of ours, which hungers and thirsts after thee, and will not be fed save with thy truth, thy justice, and thy love.

We bless thee for the glorious history which thou hast given to humankind; that from the wild babyhood wherein thou createdst man at first, thou hast led us up thus far, through devious ways, to us not understood, but known to be ordered by thee, tending to that grand destination which thou appointest for all mankind. We thank thee for the great prophets who have gone before us in every land and in every age, gifted with genius in their nature, and inspired from thee through the noble use of the talents thou gavest them. We thank thee for the truths they taught, for the justice they showed, for the love to men which was their faith and their daily life, and the piety wherein they walked and were strengthened and made glad. We bless thee for the ways of the world which were made smooth by the toil of these great men, and that we can walk serene on paths once slippery with their blood and now monumented with their memorial bones. O Lord, we thank thee for our noble brother who in many generations gone by brought so much of truth to darkling man, showed so much of justice, and lived so much of philanthropy to men and of piety to thee.

Our Father, while we thank thee for the material and the human world, we bless thee also for that divine world which transcends them both. We thank thee for that heaven, the abode of spirits disembodied from the earth, and we lift up our eyes towards those who have gone before us, our fathers, or our children, husband or wife, kinsfolk and friends, and we thank thee that we know that they are all safe with thee, thy fatherly arms around them, and thy motherly eye giving them thy blessing.

We thank thee for thyself, who fillest that world and also this globe of matter and this sphere of man with thy transcendent presence. We bless thee for thine almighty power, thine all-knowing wisdom, thine all-righteous justice, and thine all-blessing love, which watches over and saves every son and daughter of mankind. In the midst of things which we do not understand, we bless thee that we are sure of thee, and have towards thee that perfect love which casts out every fear.

We pray thee that in our soul there may be such depth of piety and such serene and tranquil trust in thee, that in our period of passion we shall tame every lust that wars against the soul, making it our servant, not our master; and in manhood's more dangerous day may we tame likewise the power of ambition, and make that our servant, to run before us and prepare the way where our laborious justice, our truth-loving wisdom, our philanthropy and our morality, with generous feet, shall tread triumphant in their journey on. May we use this world of matter to build up the being that we are to a nobler stature of strength and of beauty; and the great powers which thou hast given us, of mind, of conscience, of heart, and of soul, may we educate and culture them till we attain the measure of the stature of a perfect man, and have passed from glory to glory, till thy truth is our thought, and thy justice our will, and thy loving-kindness is the feeling of our heart, and thine own holiness of integrity is our daily life. Thus may thy kingdom come and thy will be done on earth as it is in heaven.

XXXIV.

JUNE 27, 1858.

O THOU Infinite Presence, who art everywhere, whom no name can describe, but who dwellest in houses made with hands, and fillest the heaven of heavens, which run over with thy perfections, we would draw near to thee for a moment, who forever art near to us, and would think of our own lives in the light of thy countenance, and so gird up our souls for duty and strengthen ourselves for every care and every cross thou layest on us. We know that thou needest nothing at our hands nor at our heart, but in our weakness, conscious of our infinite need of thee, we would strengthen ourselves by the prayer of a moment for the service of a day, and a week, and all our lives.

We thank thee for the world wherein thou hast cast the lines of our lot. We bless thee for the material universe where thou hast placed us. We thank thee for the heavens over our heads, purple and golden in their substance, and jewelled all over by night with such refulgent fires. We thank thee for the moon which there walks in beauty, shedding her romantic glory on the slumbering ground, and making poetic the rudest thing in country or in town. We thank thee for that great sun which brings us the day-spring from on high, and fringes the earth at morning and at evening with such evangelic beauty, and all day warms the great growing world with thy loving-kindness and thy tender mercy too. We thank thee for the earth underneath our feet, and the garment of green beauty wherewith the shoulders of the Northern world are now so sumptuously clad. We thank thee for the harvest of bread for the cattle and of bread for man, growing out of the ground, and waving in the summer wind. We thank thee for the beauty which thou enthronest in every leaf, which thou incarnatest in every little grass, and wherewith thou fringest the brooks which run among the hills, and borderest the paths which men have trod in wood and field.

We thank thee likewise for the noble nature which thou hast given to us, for this spiritual earth and heaven which we are; we thank thee for the glow of material splendor, of purple and of gold, wherewith thou investest us, and for the more than starry beauty with which our souls are jewelled forth. We thank thee for the lesser truths which walk in beauty in our infantile darkness, and the greater which in manhood's prime shed down the constant day, and fringe with morning and with evening beauty our manly life. We thank thee for the other harvests, both of beauty and of use, which grow out from the human soul, for the truths that we know, for the justice that we see, for the love that we feel to our brother-men, and all the manifold felicities we gather from the accordance of congenial souls that make sweet music on the earth. We bless thee for our dear ones, folded in our arms, sheltered underneath our roof, fed with the toil of our hands or our heads, for those who are bone of our bone and flesh of our flesh, and those others not less who are soul of our soul. We thank thee for those who daily or weekly gather with us, the benediction to our eyes, their voice the household music of our hearts, and for those also who are scattered abroad, and are of us still, though no longer with us. We thank thee for all these joys which thou givest to our earthly flesh and to our heavenly soul.

We bless thee for thyself, that we know of thine infinite perfections, thy power unending, thy justice all-righteous, thy wisdom all-knowing, and thy love which blesses and saves mankind with beatitudes which we did not know or dared not ask, and could not even dream of in our highest mood of prayer. We thank thee that while thou foldest the great universe in thine arms and carest for every system of suns and stars, not less thou feedest every little plant with sacramental cup from each cloud, holding a blessing for the trees and the grass. We thank thee that thou also watchest over the spider's nightly web spread out upon the grass, and carest for every great and every little thing, and art father and mother to all the things that be. O Lord, we thank thee that thou lovest us not only for what we are to-day, and for the small service we render to each other; but as no earthly father, as no mortal mother loves her only child, so thou lovest us, not for the service that our hands can render, or our grateful hearts in hymns of thanksgiving can ever pray, but from thine own sweet infinitude of love pourest out thine affection on Jew and Gentile, on Christian and Heathen, loving thy sinner as thou dost thy saint.

We pray thee that, so gifted, and surrounded so, and thus watched over by thy providence, we may know thee as thou art, and love thee with all our understanding and our heart and soul. May we keep the law which day by day thou writest eternally on our flesh and in our soul, and serve thee with every limb of our body, with our spirit's every faculty, and whatsoever power we gain over matter or over man. In us may there be such love and such trust in thee that we shall keep every law, do every duty, and make ourselves in thy sight as fair as the flowers on earth, or the stars in heaven. May no unclean thing stain our hands, no wicked feeling despoil us of beauty within our heart, and may we love our brothers as ourselves, and thee above all. Thus from the baby-bud whereinto we were born, may we open the great manly and womanly glory of the flower of earthly life, and bear fruit of eternal life in thy kingdom of heaven. So day by day may thy kingdom come, and thy will be done on earth as it is in heaven.

XXXV.

JULY 11, 1858.

O THOU Infinite Spirit, who dwellest in houses made with hands, and everywhere not less hast thy dwelling-place, we flee unto thee to remember before thee the joys we delight in, the duties thou givest us to do, and the sorrows we needs must bear, and in the light of thy countenance we would be strengthened for every duty, and filled with gratitude for every joy thou givest. As thou feedest the ground with sunlight from on high, and waterest it, when it askest not, from thy sacramental cup, out of the heavens, so we know that thou wilt feed and water us with thy bounty, and needest not that we should ask thee; but in our darkness we turn unto thee for light, and in our weakness, from thine infinitude we would fill our little urns with strength, and make ourselves beautiful in thy sight.

O Thou who art our Father and our Mother, we thank thee for the loving-kindness and the tender mercy which are over all thy works. We bless thee for the harvests of bread which are growing out of the ground under the incessant heat of summer, and we thank thee for the exceeding beauty wherewith thou givest thy benediction on the daily bread not less of cattle than of men. We thank thee for the transient flowers which line the way-side, and clothe the hedges and adorn the fields with heavenly magnificence, and we thank thee for all that perennial beauty which thou enthronest in the stars on high. We bless thee for the moon's romantic story, every night told to us, and the glorious loveliness of day which the sun pours out from the golden urn of thy magnificence. We bless thee that thou hast lined the borders of the sea with green and purple beauty, and scarfed the mountains with savage loveliness, and with the morning's and the evening's twofold ring of beauty thou marriest forever the day and night, revealing in this material magnificence tokens and signs of thine own loving-kindness, which passeth knowledge, and the sovereign beauty of thy spirit, which steals into our souls.

Father, we thank thee that, creating this world so great and adorning it so fair, thou hast yet made our spirit vaster than the bounds of time and space, and givest us power to adorn it with magnificence that shames the green and purple lining of the sea, and to put the stars of heaven out of sight with its sweet glory and the bravery of its spiritual loveliness. We thank thee for the great nature thou hast given us; we bless thee for its power of ceaseless progress, of continually growing greater and nobler, and fairer decked with beauty springing from the innermost of our soul. We thank thee for every triumph which mankind has won, for all the great truths which have come sounding musical from past times, for all the noble men whom in distant days thou raisedst up out of humanity, to tell us of our power, and in their lives to reveal to us so much of thyself.

We thank thee for men and women in our own time not less gifted, nor less faithful, who also speak as thou inspirest them, telling words of truth and of justice and of love, and by street-side, and in lane, and house, and everywhere, pursuing the calm and beautiful gospel of their lives, wherein they publish humanity to all mankind.

We thank thee for all that has come to us from past times and our own day. We bless thee for the special gifts thou givest to us in our several families and homes and hearts. We thank thee for the new-born life we rejoice in, and for other lives that are spared, long familiar to our eyes and our heart.

We bless thee for the various seasons of life, thanking thee for the little bud of infancy, and for the great handsome flower of manly and womanly life, fragrant with hope, and prophetic in its beauty. And not less do we thank thee for the ripened fruit of humanity; yea, we bless thee for venerable age, crowned with silver, and rich with the recollections and the beatitudes of many deeds well done. We thank thee for all the joy thou givest in this manifold human life to child and parent, to lover and beloved, to husband and wife, kinsfolk and relative and friend, and the gladsome benediction which thus thou settest on thy children's head. Yea, we thank thee that when our mortal spring has bloomed out, when our earthly summer is ended and vanished, and the ripened fruit falls from our human tree, the seed thereof thou takest to thyself to be with thee forever and forever. Yea, we thank thee for that transcendent world where thou takest to thyself the souls of all thy children, having no son of perdition, and blessing all with thine infinite fatherly and motherly love.

Remembering all these things, we pray thee that we may live great and glorious lives, full of the strength of humanity, and enriched with benedictions from thyself. May we use our bodies wisely, counting them but as the earthen vessels to hold the spiritual treasure thou givest us. In the innermost of our soul may we dwell familiar with thee, knowing all of thine infinite perfections, and so loving thee that our love shall cast out every fear, and we shall keep the law thou writest on this world of matter, and with thy still small voice proclaimest within the innermost of our soul. Day by day may we grow to higher and higher heights, and, as new-born blessings drop into our arms, as old familiar lives are spared to us, may we grow nobler and brighter by the blessings thou givest, till within us all shall be blameless, and outward everything shall be beautiful, and we shall pass from the glory of a good beginning to the greater glory of a triumphant end. So may thy kingdom come, and thy will be done on earth as it is in heaven.

XXXVI.

JULY 18, 1858.

O THOU Infinite One, who art the perpetual presence in matter and in mind, we flee unto thee, in whom we live and move and have our being, and for a moment would hold thee in our consciousness, that from the morning worship of our Sabbath day we may learn to serve thee all the days of our lives, strengthened thereby and made blessed.

We thank thee for the great world of matter, whereof thou buildest our bodies up, and whence thou feedest them continually from day to day. We thank thee for the fervent heat of summer, wherewith thou providest the food for cattle and for men, and satisfiest the wants of every plant; and we thank thee for the rain which in its season thou sheddest down on meadows newly mown, to call up new harvests where the farmer has already gathered one. We thank thee for the blessing of heat and of moisture, thy two great servants which so mysteriously create this vegetable world. We thank thee for the harvests grown or growing still out of the ground, and greatening and beautifying on many a tree. We thank thee for the bread of oxen and of men, which human toil by thy laws wins from out the ground, which thou feedest from the sun and the waters from thine own sweet heavens.

We thank thee that while thus thou ministerest unto us things that are useful, thou givest us also the benediction of beauty, not only on our own bread, but on all the food wherewith thou satisfiest the wants of every living thing. We thank thee for the great gospel of nature which thou hast writ, and revealest continually in the heavens over us, in the ground under us, and in the air whereby both we and all things continually live.

We thank thee for that greater world of spirit whereof thou buildest up our several persons, for the vast capabilities which thou givest to us, the power to know, to feel, to will, to worship, and to serve and trust. We thank thee for the power of infinite growth which thou givest to thy child mankind, and impartest also unto each of us.

We thank thee for all the blessings which have come to us from the men of times past. We bless thee for the great whom thou hast gifted with large talents and with genius, whom thou sendest from age to age to be the leaders and the guides of thy children, marshalling us the way that we should go. We thank thee for such as have brought scientific truth to light, for those who have organized into families and communities and states and nations thy multitudinous children on the earth. We bless thee for all who have taught us truth, who have shown us justice, and have revealed thyself to us in all thine infinite beauty, and have taught us to live a blameless life of love. We thank thee for thy prophets, thy evangelists, who in every tongue have spoken to mankind, doing great service to the millions who are about them, waiting for such high instruction.

We thank thee for him whom in days long since thou raisedst up in the midst of darkness to establish light, and though mankind has worshipped our brother whom we ought but to follow and to imitate, guided by his light and warned by what was ill, yet we thank thee for the great truths he proclaimed in speech, and the noble life that he lived on earth, showing us the way to thee, telling us the truth from thee, and living so much of that life that is in thee and with thee for ever and ever.

And not less do we thank thee for men with talents no smaller in our own days, who likewise serve their fellows by telling truth and proclaiming justice, and living the calm, sweet life which is piety within and philanthropic love without. We bless thee for those whose gladdening feet print the earth with the benediction of their presence, for those whose toilsome hands do good continually to mankind, and ask no return, for those whose large mind carries the lamp which is to guide mankind from Egyptian darkness to a large, fair place, where they shall dwell together in gladness and in peace; and for such as reveal to our consciousness the great truths of thine infinite goodness, power, and love, and who incarnate them in life, — O Lord, we thank thee for these, the prophets and apostles, the sages and the saints of our own day, called by whatever name, and wherever the lines of their lot be cast.

We remember before thee thine own infinite perfection, and while we thank thee for the world of matter and the world of spirit, which are thy gifts, still more do we thank thee for thyself who art the giver, folding in thy bosom other worlds of matter which we know not of, and worlds of spirit whereof we dimly learn, and whereunto with continual yearning our spirit would ascend. We thank thee for thy providence which, mid many a dark day that seems to us Egyptian night, marks the lintels of every door, and broods over every land, and with thy love comes into every household, great or small, and never departs thence, but leaves thy blessing ever fresh and ever new.

We remember our lives before thee, our several joys that we thank thee for, and yet know not how to thank thee as we ought. The sorrows thou givest us, — we dare not praise thee for them, but in their darkness and their cloud, we still thank thee that thy light comes through the darkness, and thy hand is underneath the cloud, leading us forward through them to better and more glorious things.

We remember our daily duties, how hard they often are, and we pray thee that we may use the noble faculties thou hast given us so as to bear every cross which must needs be borne, and grow greater by suffering what we needs must endure, and doing what thou commandest as our duty, and so being what thou wouldst have us be. Father we pray thee that in us there may be such knowledge of thee, such love towards thee, and such trust in thee, and such a noble pious life in ourselves, that we shall bring every limb of our body and our spirits every faculty into thy service, and so outwardly, not less than inwardly, live lives that are as fair as the lilies of the stream or the stars of heaven, and so be blameless and beautiful and acceptable in thy sight. Thus may thy kingdom come and thy will be done on earth as it is in heaven.

XXXVII.

JULY 25, 1858.

OUR Father who art in heaven, and on earth, and everywhere, we flee unto thee, and for a moment would be conscious of thy presence, and in the light of thy countenance would we remember our joys and our sorrows, our duties, our transgressions, and our hopes, and lift up to thee the glad psalm of gratitude for all that we rejoice in, and aspire towards the measure of a perfect man, and so worship thee that we shall serve thee all the days of our lives with a gladsome and accepted service. So may the prayer of our hearts be acceptable unto thee, and come out in our daily life as fair as the lilies and lasting as the stars.

O Father who art everywhere, and givest to thy creatures liberally and upbraidest not, we thank thee for the world of matter over our head and under our feet and about us on every side. We thank thee for the serene and stormy days wherewith thou equally givest thy sacrament of benediction to all things that are. We bless thee for all which the summer has thus far brought forth, for the great harvests of use which have grown alike for the cattle that serve and for imperial man who commands the things that are about him and above him and underneath his feet, and for the beauty wherewith thou broiderest every field-side and road-side, and clothest the bosom of the stream, which blossoms with fragrant loveliness. We thank thee for the great psalm of creation, where day by day, when there is no voice nor language, star speaketh unto flower, and flower speaketh unto star, and the ocean proclaims to the sky the power, the order, the mind, the loving-kindness, and the tender mercy of thy spirit, dwelling in every great and every little thing.

We thank thee for this human world whereof ourselves are a part, for the vast faculties which thou hast given us. For the fair bodies, the crown of creation, so curiously and wonderfully made, with senses which take hold of each material thing and feed thereon, converting its use and its beauty to means of human growth, we thank thee, and for this great power of mind which thou givest us, feeding alike on truth and beauty, gaining the victory over material things, making the ground, the winds and the waters, the stars and the very fire of heaven, to serve our various needs. We thank thee for this great moral power, whereby our conscience comes into accord with thine, and we know thy justice and make it our human rule of conduct, making ourselves useful to each other and acceptable to thee.

We thank thee for these generous affections which, unselfish, reach out their arms to father and mother, to kinsfolk and friend, to lover and beloved, husband and wife, parent and child, and all the great relationships wherewith the world is full. We thank thee for the greatening power of charity, which transcends the bounds of family and kindred blood, of acquaintance and congenial soul, and goes forever loving on, careful for those who are cast down, and seeking to bless with light those who are sitting benighted in the corners of the earth, to strike the fetters from the slave, to give knowledge to the ignorant, and to teach virtue and piety to men that are bowed together in their sins, in nowise able to lift themselves up.

Father we thank thee that we know thee; we bless thee for this great religious faculty, whereby we turn this world of matter and the world of soul into one great accordant psalm, and even the voices of the beasts that perish come to our ears full of religious melody, reminding us of thy providence, which is kind and large not only to angels and to men, but to the meanest thing which serves thy purpose in the world.

Father, we thank thee for that transcendent world, embracing the earth of matter and the humanity of men, that world of spirits which thou thyself inhabitest, and whereunto thou drawest thy children from year to year, as thine angel strikes off the fetters of our flesh, and clothes us with immortality. Father, we thank thee for our dear ones who have gone before us, where the mortal eye sees them not, but where the human heart knows it is well with the child, and that thou stillest the agonies of father, husband, wife or lover, with thy sweet beneficence, and art kind and merciful alike to thy saint and thy sinner. We thank thee for that other world which draws our eyes through our tears and our darkness and fills us with hope. We bless thee for thine own infinite perfection, that we can rest under the shadow of thine almighty power, thine all-knowing wisdom, thine all-righteous justice, and thine all-embracing love, which never end. O Lord, our Father and our Mother too, we know that we need not ask any good thing from thee, nor in our prayer beseech thee to remember us, for thou lovest us more than we can love ourselves, and art more desirous of our infinite welfare than we for our prosperity a single day.

We pray thee therefore that ourselves may be faithful to all the gifts which thou hast given us. Remembering thine infinite love and thy tender providence, may we put away all fear from us, and shaking off every particle of superstitious dust, may we open our souls to that glorious love which shall not be ashamed, but constrains us to keep every law which thou hast writ for us. So knowing thee and trusting thee, may we never think meanly of the nature thou hast given to us, but use these bodies as the vessels which hold the precious treasure thou hast poured therein, and with our mind and our conscience and our heart and our soul may we serve thee daily by that worship in spirit and in truth which alone achieves the great end of human destination. So using ourselves, may we wisely use the world of matter that is about us, and by our daily toil not only house and clothe and feed and medicine our flesh, but by the process thereof instruct our intellect and enlarge our conscience, fertilize our affections, and magnify this religious power that is in us. So day by day may we serve thee with perfect service, and when thou hast finished thy work with us, then, triumphant, may we journey home to be with thee, to know thee as ourselves are known, and pass from glory to glory forever and ever, entering into those joys which the eye has not seen, nor the ear heard, nor the heart of man completely known. So may thy kingdom come, and thy will be done on earth as it is in heaven.

XXXVIII.

SEPTEMBER 19, 1858.

O THOU Infinite Presence, who art everywhere, we flee unto thee for a moment, who art always near unto us. We would be conscious of thy power, thy wisdom, thy justice, and thy love, and while we feel thee most intimate at our hearts, we would remember before thee our joys and our sorrows, our hopes and our fears, whatever of virtue we have attained to, and the transgressions also wherewith we defile our soul. May the words of our mouths and the meditations of our hearts be acceptable in thy sight, O Lord, our Strength and our Redeemer.

O Thou Infinite Giver of all things, we thank thee for this great, rich world, where thou castest the lines of our lot. We thank thee for the exceeding beauty which thou hast scattered throughout the heavens and everywhere on this broad earth of thine. We thank thee that thou mouldest every leaf into a form of beauty, and globest every ripening berry into symmetric loveliness, that thou scatterest along the road-sides of the world and on the fringes of the farmer's field such wealth and luxuriance of beauty to charm our eyes from things too sensual, and slowly lift us up to what is spiritual in its loveliness and cannot pass away. We thank thee for the glory which walks abroad at night, for the moon with interchange of waxing and waning beauty, shedding her silver radiance across the darkness, for every fixed and every wandering star whose bearded presence startles us with strange and fairest light, and for the imperial sun that from his ambrosial urn pours down the day on field and town, on rich and poor, baptizing all thy world with joy. We thank thee for the ground underneath our feet, whence the various particles of our bodies are day by day so curiously taken and wonderfully framed together. We thank thee for the Spring, which brought her handsome promise, for the gorgeous preparation which the Summer made in his manly strength, and we bless thee for the months of Autumn, whose sober beauty now is cast on every hill and every tree. We thank thee for the harvests which the toil and the thought of man have gathered already from the surface of the ground, or digged from its bosom. We bless thee for the other harvests still growing beneath the earth, or hanging abundant beauties in the autumnal sun from many a tree, all over our blessed Northern land.

We thank thee likewise for this great human world which ourselves make up. We bless thee for the glorious nature which thou hast given us, for these bodies so curiously and so wonderfully made, and for this overmastering spirit which enchants into life this handful of fascinated clay. We bless thee for the large faculties which thou hast given us, and the unbounded means for development afforded in our daily toil. We thank thee for the glorious destination which thou hast set before us, appointing us our duties to do, and giving us that grand and lasting welfare which thou wilt never fail to bestow on all and each who ask it with their prayer and toil.

Father, we thank thee for the work which our hands find to do on earth. We bless thee that the process of our toil is education for our body and our mind, for our conscience and our heart and soul. We thank thee for the reward which comes as the result of our work; yea, we bless thee for the houses that we live in, for the garments that we wear, woven up of thoughtful human toil, for the bread that we eat, and the beauty that we gather from the ground, or create from the manifold material things which thou givest us.

We thank thee for those who are near and dear to us, the benediction on our daily bread, the presence of blessing in our house, and the chief ornament of our human life. We thank thee for new-born blessings which thou sendest into the arms of father and of mother, to gladden them not only, but likewise relative and friend, and to people the earth with new generations of progressive men.

Father, we remember before thee likewise that other world which transcends the earth of matter and the world of human things; we thank thee for that world which the eye hath not seen, nor the ear heard, nor the heart of man fully conceived. We bless thee for the spirits of just men made perfect who have gone before us into that kingdom of heaven, to shine like the morning stars of earth, free from all the noises which harass the world. Father, we remember before thee those dear to our hearts still, though severed from our side, and if we dare not thank thee when father or mother, when husband or wife, when son or daughter, when kinsfolk and acquaintance have their countenance changed, and they themselves are born anew into thy kingdom, we still thank thee that we are sure they are with thee, that no evil befalls the little one, or the mature one, or the aged, but the arms of thy love are about them, and thou leadest them ever forward and ever upward.

O Thou who art Infinite Perfection, we thank thee for thyself; and we know that out of thy power, thy wisdom, thy justice, and thy love, have flowed forth this world of matter, and this world of man, and that kingdom of heaven whereinto we all hope to enter at the last. We thank thee for thy loving-kindness and thy tender mercy, which are over all thy works, and where we cannot see, save through a glass darkly, we will still trust thee, with infinite longing and with absolute confidence, and that love which casteth out every fear.

Father in heaven, so gifted as we are, surrounded so, and so destined for immortal welfare, we pray thee that we may live great and noble lives on the earth, unfolding our nature day by day, using our bodies for their purpose, and the soul for its higher use, growing wiser and better as we change time into life, and daily work into exalted character. So may we live that every day we learn some new truth, practise some new virtue, and become dearer and more beautiful in thine own sight. So may thy kingdom come, and thy will be done on earth as it is in heaven.

XXXIX.

DECEMBER 5, 1858.

O THOU Infinite Spirit, who art always present, we know that we need not ask thee to remember us, and though in the weakness of our psalm we thus entreat thee, yet in the strength of our heart's prayer we know that thou needest no entreating, but rememberest us forever and forever. O Thou who art our Father, we thank thee that all day long thou hast us in thy perfect care, and when the night comes, and we lay us down, that thou still watchest over us, and givest to thy beloved even in our sleep. Father, we will not ask thee to draw nigh unto us, for thou livest and movest and hast thy being in all things that are, and most eminent in our own soul. But we will seek to draw near unto thee, that, warmed by thy fire and strengthened by thy light, from the moment of our worship, we may serve thee better all the days of our mortal life.

Father, we thank thee for thyself. We bless thee that thou createdst us and all things from thy perfect love, and preappointed us all to infinite and eternal welfare, and in the world about us and the world within didst wonderfully provide the means thereto, so that our follies even shall help us, and the wrath of man shall serve thy great purpose, and the remainder of wrath thou wilt restrain. O Lord, who art our Father and our Mother too, we thank thee that thy love never fails, that though our mortal friends perish from out our sight, though father and mother may forget us, and we be faithless to our own selves, yet thou never leavest, nor forsakest, nor art unfaithful, but lovest us far more than we are able to ask, or even to think or to wish in the extreme of our heart.

We bless thee for the world thou hast given us all around. We thank thee for the Summer's beauty that has passed, leaving behind her the autumnal grain, and the rich and bountiful fruits of harvest. And now that the Winter is upon us, we bless thee for this angel whom thou hast sent down to clothe the earth in white raiment, and adorn it with loveliness, this garment of snow which thou so sweetly administerest out of thy heavens to all these Northern lands, which hang on thy bounty and are fed from thy never-ending love.

We thank thee for all the blessings which we have inherited from ages gone before us. We bless thee for so much of civilization as has fallen to our lot, for the noble institutions which our fathers builded up with their prayer and their toil, with their sword and their blood. We thank thee for every wise thing in our government which has come down to us, for all the excellence which is in our social organizations, for the friendly affection which adorns our household and our home. We thank thee for those schools of the people where thou instructest thy children from day to day; we bless thee for the sweet influences which proceed thence and enrich mankind, while they instruct and lift us up. We thank thee for all the good there is in the churches called after thy name; we bless thee for all the various denominations on the earth, thanking thee that their several faith — whether Heathen, or Greek, or Jew, or Christian — is to them of such infinite worth. We bless thee for all of truth which we may have gathered from the various religions of the world, and most of all for what we have learned of thyself, in the calm and still communing of our own heart with thee. We thank thee that thou inspirest all of thy children, who, with open mind and obedient heart, flee unto thee, seeking for truth, for justice, for love, and the sweet piety which so adorns and beautifies the inner man.

We bless thee for the dear ones whom affection joins to our heart, bone of our bone, flesh of our flesh, or joined by a still nearer and more delicious kindred of the soul. O Lord, we remember the friendships which time and distance cannot sever, we remember the love of kinsfolk and acquaintance, whom death only hides from our eye, but does not take from our heart. We thank thee for the just ones made perfect who have gone from us, and those who in their imperfection have been translated, for we know that thou placest them in the line of advancement, and leadest them ever upwards, and still further on.

We remember the great duties which are before us, incumbent on such natures and so large an inheritance and such ample opportunity for toil. We remember before thee with shame and confusedness of heart our own weakness, our folly and our pride, and the manifold transgressions wherewith we sin against our body or our soul, against thy goodness, O thou Infinite Mother, who holdest us in thy hand, and warmest us with the breath of thy love. And we pray thee that we may put away every folly, and be greatly chastised for every wrong, till, penitent therefor, we turn from it, and, though with bleeding feet, tread the paths of righteousness, leading us to peace and gladness and joy of soul.

Father, we will not pray thee for this world's goods; we know not of these things how to pray thee as we ought; therefore we dare not ask thee for riches or for poverty, for length of life, nor for shortness of days. But we pray thee that we may so toil in our various lot that we grow wiser and better, that we have a sure and abiding sense of thy goodness, thy power, and thy love, and of the great and noble nature thou hast given us, and the glorious destination thou hast prepared. Then may our hands work out our own salvation, with joy and with gladness then may we toil for our brother men; and our poor and humble lives, — may they enrich and magnify the age we live in. Thus day by day may we serve thee, and so may thy kingdom come and thy will be done on earth as it is in heaven!

XL.

JANUARY 2, 1859.

O THOU who art everywhere, whom no eye can see, but every heart can feel, we flee unto thee, and for a moment would hold thee in our consciousness, who art not far from any one of us, but always hast us in thy care and keeping, watching over and doing us good. We would remember before thee our joys and our sorrows, our hopes and our fears, our good deeds and our transgressions, and while we meditate thereon, may we be penitent for every wrong deed, and greatly ashamed of all wickedness, but filled with noble aspirations, which shall bear us up to higher and higher heights of human excellence. O Thou who art ever near us, may thy spirit pray with us in our prayer, teaching us the things we ought to pray for, and strengthening us mightily in the inner man.

O Thou Infinite Spirit, we thank thee for all thy loving-kindness and thy tender mercy, which gave us our being first, and lengthenest out our lives from day to day, and from year to year, while thou presentest before us the immortal life, which eye has not seen, nor ear heard, nor our frail hearts completely understood.

We thank thee for this fair sunlight which gladdens and cheers the faces of men, while it fills up with handsomeness the wintry hour. We thank thee for the stars, which all night long keep shining watch above a sleeping world; and we bless thee for thy providence, which cares for us when we slumber, and when we wake. Yea, we thank thee that underneath thy care we can lay us down and sleep in safety, and when we wake we are still with thee.

While we stand at the entrance of a new year, remembering thy presence with us, we cast our eyes backward, and we thank thee for all the joy and the gladness which came to our lot in the months that are past. We thank thee for the health and energy that have been in our earthly frame. We bless thee for the work our hands found to do, for the joy which comes from the harvested result of our toil and thought, and that greater but unasked joy and blessedness which comes from the education which the process of our daily toil in thy marvellous providence doth bring about.

Father, we thank thee for the new ties of mortal love which we have formed on earth, whereby eyes behold light in mutual eyes, and hearts that once were twain become one. We thank thee for the new-born blessings, these little messiahs which thy loving-kindness has left in many an earnest home. We bless thee for all the joys which spring from the various affections of life, which set the solitary in families, and of twain make one, and thence bring manifold life to increase and multiply and gladden the world.

Father, we remember before thee the sorrows and disappointments with which we have sometimes been tried. We remember the dear ones whom thou hast taken from our mortal arms, whose countenance thou hast changed, and whom thou hast sent away; and though we have not always been strong enough to understand thy providence, or to welcome the hand which took, as that which gave, yet we thank thee that through the darkness that surrounded us we can see a great and marvellous light, whereunto we are marching step by step, whither our dear ones are gone before, not lost, but found in thee. O Father on earth, Father in heaven, Father and Mother too, we thank thee for that other world whither so many of our friends are gone, and whither our own faces are also set. We thank thee that we are conscious of our immortality, and sure that when we drop the body we are clothed upon with immortal life, and pass from glory to glory, in a progress which can never end.

We remember before thee the sins and transgressions which we have often committed; we remember the wrong deeds that we have done, the unholy feelings that we have cherished, and the wicked thoughts which have sometimes come into our minds, and been bidden to rest and tarry there. O Lord, full of pain and sadness for every wrong deed we have done, for the unholy words we have spoke, and the wicked feelings we have nourished in us, we pray thee that we may not be cast down by our penitence, but ashamed of our transgression, and warned by our fall, walk more heedfully in times that are to come, and journey from strength to strength, our hands uplifted, and our hearts sustained by thee.

O Thou who knowest what all time shall bring forth, we cast our eyes forward, and though every day is hidden in darkness before our eyes, we pray thee that there may be such light within our heart, that it shall make it all glorious light about us, from hour to hour, and in the strength that thou givest us may we do the appointed duty of each day, and reverently bear its cross, and so fill up all our time with thy service. Within us may the true religion find its temple and its home; may thy great truths dwell in us, and the noble feelings of love to each other, and unchanging and perfect love to thee; here may they live and do their perfect work; may they bring down every high thought which exalts itself unduly, may they tame every unworthy passion, and change our ambition from evil into good, so that all our days shall be thy days, our prayer thy worship, and our life thy continual service, and all our earthly days be made gladsome and glorious in thy sight. Then, when thou hast finished thy work with us on earth, may we lift up our eyes towards thee with gladness and great joy, and go home to that world where all tears are wiped from every eye, and where sorrow and sighing shall come no more, but we shall shine in the light of thy love, and pass from glory to glory.

Our Father who art in heaven, hallowed be thy name. May thy kingdom come, and thy will be done on earth as it is done in heaven. Give us each day our daily bread. Forgive us our trespasses as we forgive those who trespass against us. Lead us not into temptation but deliver us from its evil. For thine is the kingdom and the power and the glory forever. Amen.

THE END.

CAMBRIDGE: PRINTED BY H. O. HOUGHTON.

www.ingramcontent.com/pod-product-compliance
Lightning Source LLC
LaVergne TN
LVHW011214110826
845150LV00006B/1432

* 9 7 8 1 4 2 5 5 1 7 3 4 2 *